SUCCESSFUL WRITING

STARTING TO
WRITE

How to create written work for
publication and profit

Marina &
Deborah Oliver

How To Books

Cartoons by Mike Flanagan

British Library Cataloguing-in-Publication data
A catalogue record for this book is available from the British Library.

First published in 1996 by How To Books Ltd, Plymbridge House,
Estover Road, Plymouth PL6 7PZ, United Kingdom.

Note: The material contained in this book is set out in good faith for
general guidance and no liability can be accepted for loss or expense
incurred as a result of relying in particular circumstances on statements
made in the book. The laws and regulations are complex and liable to
change, and readers should check the current position with the relevant
authorities before making personal arrangements.

Produced for How To Books by Deer Park Productions

Typeset by Concept Communications, Crayford, Kent.
Printed and bound in Great Britain by The Cromwell Press,
Broughton Gifford, Melksham, Wiltshire.

Contents

List of Illustrations

Preface

This book answers the fundamental questions of how a writer gets started, manages the process of writing, and becomes effective. It saves new writers years of possible floundering. You need not waste time and resources following unreasonable objectives or being unable to find the right niche.

If you are just starting as a writer this book will help you to examine your motivations, devise your aims, explore different methods and possibilities until you find the one which suits you best. There are many tips which it may have taken others years to find. You will discover how to research the market and send your work to appropriate publishers. You will learn how to find, organise, and use ideas effectively, how to perfect your work, and give it the best possible chance of selling.

Starting to Write should be invaluable both for people who have never before considered writing for profit, and for those who have started but found it more of a maze than they expected.

Marina Oliver and Deborah Oliver

1
Getting Started

TAKING THE OPPORTUNITY

You can write at any age. People of 80 have published first novels, or are writing newspaper columns. It has always been a practical, part-time career for people who have to work at odd times or from home: shift-workers and mothers of young children.

With early retirement and longer life expectancy writing can be a second (or third or fourth) career.

Writing can produce useful extra income, although great fame and fortune will come only to a few — but people can enjoy singing in a choir without aiming to become world-renowned opera stars.

There are many valid reasons for writing

● Many people have a vague, undirected desire to write, but don't know how to start.

● Others have a burning message to communicate but are unsure of how or where to do this.

● Perhaps you enjoy writing letters and would like to expand.

● English was your best subject at school and you want to hone your skill.

● Often we read published articles, plays or books and believe we could do better.

● Maybe you want to leave a record of your life and times for your grandchildren.

● Writing about fears and worries can help to dispel them.

● A polemical letter can dissipate a feeling of helpless rage.

● You may have drawers or files full of notes, essays, scenes, conversations, chapters of books, and have no idea what to do with them.

Checklist: Reasons for wanting to write

1. Money.
2. Fame.
3. Publication.
4. As a hobby.
5. For your grandchildren.
6. Therapy.
7. You were good at composition at school.

Action points

1. Decide where or how would you like to see your work published (*eg* books, magazines, radio).

2. List any writing you have done in the past, for a hobby as opposed to work. Think back to school or since, and say which types of writing you were better at than others.

LOOKING AT THE OPTIONS

Likes
You will probably choose to write what you enjoy reading (or listening to or watching — but for the sake of brevity the term 'read' will include radio, theatre and television media). This is partly due to a sense of familiarity, partly instinctive.

Select your strong points
Consider your strengths and ask whether you might try another form.

● If you are exceptionally good at writing dialogue you might try drama as well as novels.

● If you have a deep knowledge of something, whether it be model trains or computer software, you could write articles for specialist magazines.

- If you can explain things to non-experts, you could write general articles or a textbook.

FACTUAL OR CREATIVE?

Writing non-fiction
There are many opportunities to write non-fiction. You could try the following:

- books of ideas (*eg* on business or politics)
- practical books (*eg* on carpentry or tapestry work)
- newspaper reports
- magazine or newspaper articles
- radio talks or documentaries
- television documentaries
- textbooks for schools/colleges
- guide books
- illustrated books for children.

Use it again
A non-fiction idea can be used in many different forms:

- What is wrong for an article may work as a radio talk.

- A series of articles might make a book.

- You could produce two articles explaining something to different readers — let's say on medical matters such as a new treatment or drug. The first article could be a technical one aimed at doctors, the second in general terms explaining symptoms or techniques for patients.

Can you create fiction?
Fiction has many opportunities. A simple idea might start as a short story, be converted into a play or expanded by the addition of more characters and sub-plots into a novel.

Narrative fiction includes:

- novels
- short stories

- stories for children
- photo-stories.

Drama includes:

- theatre plays
- pantomime
- radio plays
- radio serials
- television plays
- television serials
- film scripts.

There is also poetry plus:

- lyrics
- jingles for advertisements.

Try them out
All these different types demand different techniques. Try out different forms until you discover which one works best for you.

Action points

1. Look at how radio, stage and television plays differ.

2. Say which forms of writing you have never considered but now might want to try, and why.

WRITING WHAT YOU KNOW

When people are advised to write about what they know they can panic, think they know nothing special, important or interesting to others. This is nonsense — we all have some knowledge.

You know a lot
Almost everyone knows something about cooking or gardening. Cookery and gardening books and magazines are very popular. The difference between a cook and a writer of successful cookery books is that the latter writes about it, and does so with originality.

Or you can research it

Writers have often simply collected information in a structured way, perhaps experimented, and then organised the information they want to pass on in an interesting, saleable form.

You don't need to be an expert

A news reporter must clarify facts for the reader, and these facts may be new to the journalist. He needs to learn enough not to say something stupid or totally false, but he doesn't need to be an expert. A writer has to research his subjects. **Write about what you know or can research**.

Imagination is important too

If you write historical novels or fantasy it must by its very nature be about something you have not experienced. Crime novelists are not all murderers or detectives. Imagination and research are essential in all forms of writing, to add to, flesh out, or make bare facts interesting.

Checklist: Look at what you know

1. What paid jobs have you done?

2. What jobs have you done about the home?

3. What voluntary jobs have you done?

4. What are your hobbies?

5. What sports are you interested in?

6. What countries or places have you travelled to?

7. Have you a retentive memory for culture, accents, or dialects?

8. What do you have strong opinions about?

9. What experts do you know?

10. What subjects can you easily get information about?

WRITING IS A CRAFT

Sloppiness of expression and inattention to detail are anathema to publishers and discerning readers.

Practice is essential

No one expects to play a piano concerto without long hours of practice. Writing success involves learning and developing techniques, applying discipline, constant practising and seeking for perfection.

Occasionally a novice becomes an overnight bestselling novelist, but most writers undergo a long process of learning, and a gradual climb part-way up the ladder.

Study the market

Many excellent pieces of writing fail to find publishers.

The writer may have sent it to the wrong place or at the wrong time, or been unlucky because a publisher liked but could not use it.

To make money you must provide what is in demand. It's a waste of time writing a three-hour radio play when broadcasters only produce 30, 60 or 90 minute plays.

Action point

Decide what you can do if your first efforts towards publication are not successful.

EXPLORING DIFFERENT METHODS

You can approach a project by:

- working it all out in your head beforehand
- writing a few notes first
- writing detailed notes first
- writing a summary or synopsis first
- beginning to write and seeing where it takes you
- constantly redrafting as you go
- redrafting after finishing a first attempt.

Try them out

Try out different methods. This learning process will make future writing easier and more efficient.

In a novel you can start with a situation and characters and let them take over, going where they choose. A textbook will have to be planned more precisely and may have to conform to a series for length, number of sections, and style. A radio or TV script has to fit a specified time slot.

For a short story or magazine article you need to know which magazine it is aimed at. This is because the length, style, type of reader and arrangement will differ for each.

CASE STUDIES

Yvonne starts with a summary

Yvonne teaches the reception class and spends a great deal of time preparing for her four and five-year-olds. She is always well prepared for her class, knowing what she means to do all day long. She decides to write stories for them, but after a while she finds she doesn't know what to put next or how the story will develop.

A friend suggests that every time she has an idea she tries to do a brief outline of the plot, then she won't get stuck.

This method works for Yvonne, and she begins to write lots of children's stories.

Susan rushes in

Susan wants to write a book about bringing up children. After all, she's had three herself.

She begins to write it one evening, and spends several days writing odd bits and pieces as the topics occur to her. By the end of a week she has a folder full of notes but no clear idea of how she is going to structure her book.

'I don't know whether to deal with children by age, say a chapter for each year, or by particular problems such as not eating,' she says gloomily. 'What I've done so far doesn't fit into any pattern; I'll have to start again.'

Susan was in too much of a hurry to start. She should have thought more about it first.

James makes a detailed plan

James has been retired for six months and is becoming bored with golf and gardening. 'I need something to occupy my mind,' he tells his wife.

'What about that book on management techniques you never had time to write before?'

'Yes. I'll start collecting my ideas straight away.'

'Before you start, can you mend the leak under the sink? And you promised to look at the bedside lamp in the spare bedroom, see why it keeps flickering.'

In between DIY jobs James writes down his ideas, sorts out the plan of a book, and soon has a folder full of detail.

He is half way towards writing his book.

DISCUSSION POINTS

1. Write down your very first idea for a writing project, and decide what form of writing it is suited for — novel, article, drama. Do you think this sort of writing will be what you always do, and for what reasons?

2. Make notes for your first idea, including how you will begin and end, and briefly what you will include. Does this preparation help you to expand the idea, and if so why do you think this is?

3. If your first idea was for fiction try to use it in a non-fiction form. If for non-fiction, try to place it in a fictional story. Does this sort of exercise expand your views of how you can use ideas?

2
Collecting the Tools

Being organised is an aid to the writing process.

MAKING A PLACE OF YOUR OWN

This isn't absolutely essential but it helps enormously, even if it is just a small table in your bedroom.

You could create a special alcove with screens or rearranged furniture. Consider converting an attic or the cupboard under the stairs (but make sure you have sufficient ventilation!). With adequate heating a garden shed or outhouse might be usable.

Action point

Make a list of essentials and decide how much shelf or drawer space you need to keep them in.

Keep it to yourself

Once you have such a space make it sacrosanct! However small it is, try to arrange vital reference books, paper and notes within reach. Include a comfortable chair and good lighting.

You may need peace to operate. Make it clear to everyone that writing is a job, and interruptions damage the creative process. You need mental as well as physical space.

ORGANISING YOUR TIME

Different methods suit different writers. Personal circumstances such as children or jobs may limit such decisions. It may be possible to write only at weekends, or to find time only by giving up other activities. The important thing is to find a routine which fits your circumstances, and to write regularly. Keep a 'writing diary' to help you see what is your most productive time (see Figure 1).

Finding the best time

Many writers have set times for writing, every morning or afternoon, or from 9.00 am to 6.00 pm six days a week.

Others spend however long it takes to write four or five hundred or a thousand words each day.

Some write as long as they physically can when ideas are flowing, or set deadlines for completing a chapter, book or article.

WRITING DIARY

Date	Starting time	Finishing time	No of words/pages
Jan 1	3.00 pm	6.30 pm	1,000 words
Jan 2	6.00 pm	8.30 pm	500 words
Jan 3	6.00 pm	7.00 pm	half a page
Jan 4	2.00 pm	5.00 pm	1,000 words

Fig. 1. A sample writing diary.

Choose the best time for you

The time of day may depend on whether you are a lark or an owl. Many writers get up early and write before they go to work. Others work when everyone else is in bed. Some write during lunch breaks.

Some days other commitments make even half an hour impossible. It helps to aim for a set number of hours or words per week. If one day or week is exceptionally busy, make up the time later — or in advance.

Be realistic

Don't aim too high at first. If you fail to keep a too-demanding schedule you may well become disheartened and give up.

You don't need a pen to 'write'

The term 'writing' can be misleading. It isn't just the time spent with a pen or keyboard. You need:

- to think
- to make notes
- to do research
- or revise what is already written.

Established writers have to read proofs and attend press and publicity events.

These are necessary aspects of writing, and if they cut into your 'writing time' don't worry. The chances are you will be thinking or researching outside your allotted hours anyway.

Time spent going on trains, walking the dog, or mowing the lawn can be used productively.

Checklist: Decide when and what you can manage

1. How good are you at managing your time?

2. Do you need to discipline yourself to manage your free time profitably?

3. Will you set aside a special time each day?

4. If so, what time of day is most practicable?

5. Are you a lark or an owl?

6. Will you set aside a special time each week?

7. If so, which day and what time?

8. How many hours per week can you realistically devote to writing?

Action points

1. Decide how long you can write for each week, and set a deadline for your first project.

2. Keep records of the time set aside to write and of what is achieved.

ORGANISING YOUR SPACE

Do you have adequate storage space for paper, notes, reference books, manuscripts and magazines? Eventually you will need far more than your first estimates of:

● bookshelves

- desk drawers
- filing cabinets
- cupboards.

It helps to have the most frequently used reference books close to hand, but you don't need everything in or by your desk.

It's luxurious to have every variety of sophisticated office storage facility, but you can do it cheaply or improvise.

Improvisation

- You can make bookshelves with bricks and planks to fit awkward places.

- To store hanging or envelope files get appropriate sized, strong and deep cardboard boxes from supermarkets.

- You can make dividers from sheets of stiff cardboard, or make folders with large old envelopes or paper bags.

- Label everything prominently.

- Buy typing or computer paper in boxes of 500 or 2,000 sheets. This is cheaper, and the boxes make ideal trays or storage containers.

Efficiency

Devise a filing system early on. You may file alphabetically, or keep notes on various subjects separate from letters or notes about markets. You will need a method of keeping track of your submissions, and of earnings and expenses (see Figure 2). Two handy notebooks may be the easiest for this.

Start simply

A complicated system is confusing and time wasting. As you collect reference material and notes you can expand to cater for developing needs.

File your notes regularly, in too many rather than too few separate files.

Action points

1. Work out how to improve storage space yet have information and books accessible.

2. Think out the best filing system for your first projects.

Taxing matters

When you are earning, equipment and essential materials like postage and books for reference can be tax-deductible. It is worth talking to your tax office. In any case keep receipts. Registration for VAT is unlikely at first.

	SUBMISSION CHECKLIST	
	Project A	**Project B**
item	Article babycare	Proposal for babycare article
date sent	Jan 1/96	Feb 2nd
postage	25p	25p
to	Blooming Baby	KiddyKare
date responded	Jan 31/96	Feb 10/96
date chased		
result	rej	send
notes	no unsolicited material taken	want shorter

Fig. 2. You will need a submission checklist.

PRACTICAL AIDS

Typing

Many writers start with pen or pencil. With pencils you can erase and change, but eventually a script must be typed. Publishers insist on this, however clear your handwriting.

A professional typing agency is expensive. It will be much cheaper and probably quicker to learn to type.

Computers

If you need to buy a typewriter see if you can afford a word processor or computer. Often extra copies are needed, and it is cheaper to print again than photocopy. Carbon copies are only acceptable for your own use.

A personal computer can also be used for making notes, keeping diaries, doing accounts, drawing diagrams or graphs, communicating with information agencies or other computers over telephone lines. The software, or programs, provide these facilities.

Printers
A small computer and simple word processing program may be enough for you, but good print quality is important. You can skimp on the computer but buy the best printer you can afford.

Books and magazines
Writers need all sorts of books:

General reference books
General reference books are invaluable. Second hand copies are often perfectly adequate. It's amazing how often writers need to consult dictionaries for the exact meanings of words, or Roget's Thesaurus for slightly different or more precise words.

You may want specialised dictionaries such as historical slang, modern slang, synonyms etc. An American dictionary helps if you want to sell in the States. A spelling dictionary is quicker when all you want to check is a spelling.

You'll probably want books on grammar, a small encyclopaedia, and an atlas to provide valuable information such as time zones and weather patterns.

Specific reference books
Other books worth collecting, especially by fiction writers, are dictionaries of quotations, telephone directories (for names of characters), books of names, books on furniture, costume, and houses, second hand copies of *Who's Who?* and *Whitaker's Almanack*, hotel and tourist guides, and maps.

You will probably have books on subjects which interest you and know about the standard reference sources. You will need to consult reference books in libraries, but it is convenient to have frequently used books at home. For reference books on new subjects, and a quick overall view, books for children are useful.

Checklist: Which of the following do you already have?

- dictionary
- spelling dictionary
- a book on grammar

- thesaurus
- encyclopaedia
- world atlas
- road gazetteer.

Checklist: Do you have special reference books for your own subjects?

- historical
- geographical
- political
- technical
- business
- DIY
- other.

Action point
Decide which books you need and how you might obtain them.

Yearbooks for writers
The Writer's Handbook and *The Writers' and Artists' Yearbook* are updated annually, and as the publishing scene changes often it is worth getting as recent an edition as possible. They give addresses of publishers and agents, names of editors, the sort of material they want and an indication, sometimes, of how much magazines pay.

They save time and effort by indicating whether a complete manuscript or a preliminary letter is requested. They also give details of societies and prizes.

Handbooks for writers
If you want to write for magazines or radio, travel articles, crime or historical fiction, there will be an advice manual on how to set about it, full of specific hints.

Magazines for writers
Writers News, Writing, Writers' Monthly and *Writers' Forum* carry useful articles on all aspects of writing, about people — writers and publishers — plus information on competitions and advertisements for many services.

Publishing News and *The Bookseller* are the trade organs for book publishing. *Media Week, The Publisher*, and *Publishing* are more for the magazine publishing trade. They are worth consulting in libraries for an overview of what is being published and by which firms, who the editors are, which firms are profitable, and lots of other useful information. See the list of magazines at the end of the book.

Action point
Could you ask someone for books or a magazine subscription as a birthday or Christmas gift? Or could you share a subscription with a fellow writer?

SUPPORT GROUPS

Networking
Talking and being with others in the same profession inspires ideas and confidence. It also provides tips on markets. Getting to know other writers can give you valuable contacts.

Joining a group
You could join a local or national group, or a creative writing class. You might attend day, weekend or longer courses. You could take a correspondence course. You do not have to be alone.

Local groups meet in homes or public halls. Libraries and local papers will have details. Some cater for all interests or just one, such as poetry.

Most have evenings of reading and discussing manuscripts. These can be useful for receiving the opinions of others and meeting fellow writers to discuss common problems. Groups sometimes have outside speakers — editors, agents or other writers, which is a good opportunity to ask questions and begin to network.

Try a couple of meetings first. Make sure you have the same objectives as the rest of the group.

Action point
Explore the possibility of joining the following groups:

- local general group
- local specific group (*eg* poetry circle)
- local critique group
- postal critique group
- national specialist group
- national general group.

National
Many published writers belong to the **Society of Authors**. The **Crime Writers' Association** admits only published crime writers. The **Romantic Novelists' Association** has a scheme for giving critiques to unpublished new writers. The **British Fantasy Society** is open to non-writers. Details of others are in the yearbooks.

Creative writing classes
These are usually run by the local education authority, and libraries have details. They can be for the beginner, may be a continuing course where people attend for several years, and can even be university and post-graduate level.

Some may be for particular areas of writing, but most are general. Try to sample a class before spending time and money.

Attending awaydays

Dayschools, weekend or week courses can be fun and provide opportunities to meet top people. They can be talks or workshops and are advertised in magazines for writers.

Many are for specific types of writing; the bigger ones are festivals with numerous activities going on at the same time. There are lectures, courses you can take, and lots of opportunities for congenial shop talk. At literary festivals you can listen to and meet writers. The value of listening to practising writers is hearing how they work, picking up hints, seeing different ways to do things.

Distance learning

Correspondence courses are valuable for people who cannot attend classes or who wish to work at their own pace. They are usually specific to one kind of writing. You will get personal tuition but at a distance. Good courses are organised so that you can be doing the next lesson while awaiting the return of the last. Choose colleges recognised by a professional body such as The Council for the Accreditation of Correspondence Colleges.

CASE STUDIES

Yvonne joins a class

Yvonne decides that her stories are too similar to the ones already in children's books, so she would try stories for adults. She reads some books, but that doesn't seem to help: they don't tell her whether she is getting it right.

She wonders whether a correspondence course would be good for her, but she enjoys being with people, and wants to be able to ask more questions and get answers straight away.

'I'm going to a yoga class at the adult education centre,' a fellow teacher says. 'They have a creative writing class on the same evening. Why don't you come?'

Yvonne joins the class, and finds that the regular exercises keep her busy and give her lots of ideas for different types of writing.

Susan loses her way

Susan abandons her childcare book but is determined to succeed as a writer. She has a friend Mary who writes novels, but she wants to try something different.

By the end of the week she has bought a dozen books about various types of writing. She reads and scribbles down ideas while the family watch TV. She begins several short stories and articles, and a radio play, but she is always having to clear them away to do other jobs. The pages get muddled and she becomes more and more frustrated.

Susan hasn't stopped to think, to discover what she wants and can write about, or to organise her time or space.

James looks for the experts

James's book is rejected, his ideas are out of date, so he decides to try articles instead. He sets up a desk and filing cabinet, and joins a class. They all want to write fiction.

'That's no good for me. I don't have any imagination.'

'Try a correspondence course.'

'That would take too long.'

Then James sees in the local paper that a journalist is coming to talk to a local writers' group. He asks if he could go along.

The group welcomes him, and he comes home full of ideas for different sorts of writing he could try.

James looked for practical help to suit his own needs.

DISCUSSION POINTS

1. Step back from your writing corner and take a good look at it for ten minutes. Try to imagine possible changes. Is it organised in the best possible way for your current needs, and can you predict how it might need to be changed in the future?

2. Collect all your notes which are on separate sheets of paper and spread them out in about five or six piles, roughly by type — ideas, addresses, tips, and so on. Can you sub-divide the piles even more, and does this help to start off a filing system in a way you will find helpful?

3. In a small notebook make lists of reference and writing books you already have, then add books you would like to buy or read, either ones you already know about or others you may see in the library or bookshop. How will this help you in your writing plan?

3
Researching Your Market

IT ISN'T DIFFICULT

The word research conjures up visions of academics delving into dusty manuscripts in libraries. For a writer it's different. There are two main areas of research.

- The first involves **finding out about publishers** and what they want, and that is what we'll be talking about in this chapter.

- The second comes later, and consists of looking at places, talking to people, and reading other books. It is the **searching out of facts and opinions**, or the verification of facts, to use them in a piece of writing. It involves covering all shades of opinion for a balanced view.

LOOKING IN BOOKSHOPS

If you want to write novels, you need to know what is currently being published and what is popular. Publishers like to buy scripts that fit into categories — romance, science fiction, or literary — because that makes them easier to market.

The best place to find new books is not a library. They will have a small choice and the new books are probably on loan. Go to a big book-shop.

Researching the fiction market
Bookshops first

- Go to a large bookshop, *eg* W H Smith.

- Ignore the hardbacks, which will be a limited selection of best sellers.

● Look at paperbacks, especially new and best sellers.

● Look along the sections of popular or crime or 20th century fiction, whichever interests you most.

● Read the blurbs on the backs of the books to see what sort of stories are currently popular. You will find quite a few similarities.

● Note which publishers are most often represented. Many publishers specialise in particular types of books.

● Note which authors have several titles displayed, since they will be the most popular whose books are always in demand.

By this time you will have a lot of notes, but you can then move to a library.

Action point
Make a list of at least a dozen authors in your chosen field or fields, with the titles of their most recent three or four books, dates of publication, and publishers, in both hard and paperback.

Non-fiction books
Use the same system as for fiction. As non-fiction books tend to be available for longer than most fiction titles, libraries will carry a larger selection of older but still useful titles. You will probably obtain more comprehensive information there.

SURVEYING MAGAZINES

You can write fiction, short stories or serials for many magazines, but most of their contents are non-fiction articles.

If you aim to write for magazines go to a newsagent who stocks a wide selection of magazines. Look at the titles and contents.

Magazine categories
There are ten main categories of magazines, and sub-sections within them:

1. **Provincial**, covering a town or county or area, and usually monthly or quarterly, often delivered free to homes within the area or as a supplement to a local newspaper.

2. **General interest** magazines which are read by many people.

3. Magazines aimed either at **women or men**, with a broad range of contents. There are dozens of weekly and monthly titles, with a wide variety of readership.

4. **Teenage** magazines, often story magazines, catering for different ages.

5. Magazines for **children**, from pre-school ages to early teens. These may be strip comic papers or serious, educational titles.

6. **Hobby** magazines. It sometimes seems that if there is any sort of hobby there will be at least one magazine devoted to it.

7. **Specialist** magazines which might overlap with the other categories, but perhaps be less general than the second category and more detailed than a basic hobby magazine. There are also various advertising magazines with thousands of small ads, or details about commodities like cars.

8. **Trade** magazines cater for people in particular jobs and industries, and are more likely to be sold on subscription than found in a newsagent's display.

9. **Sports** magazines which can overlap with hobbies.

10. **Weekly comment**, usually on politics or the arts or world affairs.

If you know already what sort of subjects you would like to tackle, you need to take a closer look at several magazines which deal with them, and narrow down your targets. Then study a few magazines in depth for several issues. There are tips on how to do this in the next chapter.

Action point
Think of an article topic, and make a list of at least six magazines which might be interested. Keep this list for further work in Chapter 4.

FINDING GAPS IN THE MARKET

It can be hard work
There is no short-cut to finding a niche you could fill. The competition

for existing ones is intense, so you will have to work hard researching the possibilities.

Gaps may be illusory

There may appear to be obvious gaps in what a publisher produces, or what is in a magazine. If you find what looks to be a gap, ask some questions:

● Is this publisher a different kind of specialist, who does not publish school textbooks or books on railway history?

● If there are no historical sagas set in the tenth century BC, might this be because there is little demand for them?

● If this magazine does not contain short stories, is it the policy of the publisher?

● There are no long in-depth articles in this magazine. Is this because it is aimed at a readership which wants short snappy pieces rather than closely argued academic essays?

Looking for reasons

You may find the answers to these questions in writers' yearbooks or magazines. You will not be able to change a publisher's policy, but you may find genuine gaps.

Keep your eyes and ears open

● There may be requests in writing magazines for particular types of books and articles.

● You may, through networking, hear of opportunities.

● A new publisher or a new magazine editor or a new editor of an old magazine will perhaps be more ready to consider new contributors than well-established ones who already have known contributors.

● The less well-known magazines will receive fewer submissions, so your chances of acceptance are higher with these.

Always be on the alert for opportunities, and ready to exploit them.

USING LIBRARIES

Read the fiction

It is bad for the pockets of publishers and authors to advise you to borrow instead of buy books, but far better for your finances.

You may be able to buy recent titles in second hand shops, market stalls or charity shops, but the surest way of finding a particular title is to order it through a library.

If your library does not have a particular book the librarians ought to be able to find it for you through the Inter-Library Loan Scheme.

If you aim to write novels you will need to read hundreds rather than dozens of books.

Checklist: How to do fiction market research

1. Read all you can of popular authors and the other books their publishers deal with.

2. Don't just read, analyse as described in Chapter 4.

3. Consult *The Guardian* annual list of the top hundred fast sellers, which is another way of discovering who the most popular authors are.

4. Read *The Bookseller* review columns and study adverts from publishers you have already pinpointed as doing your sort of books.

Study the non-fiction

Ask for help

Librarians are normally happy to help track down facts or books and can suggest ways to look for more information.

●   Have you ever looked something up in a book?

●   Have you ever asked a librarian for help in finding a book on a certain topic?

For any particular topic, search the library for:

●   subject index
●   bibliography of books and pamphlets
●   periodicals via an index.

Don't forget general reference books and encyclopaedias which will often give reading lists or references.

Specialist libraries

If your research involves very specific information, you may find the ordinary reference library cannot supply it. They should, however, be able to tell you about specialist libraries where you might find what you want. Museums are also useful sources of information.

Action point

Keep a list of any possible sources of information in your area, specialist libraries and museums, and try to visit them and make notes on what sort of material they have available.

USING SPECIALISTS

All sorts of people have specialist knowledge

● Have you ever asked your neighbours or friends or relatives for information?

● Have you ever asked a public or private organisation for information?

Using an agent

Agents are specialists. Employing one is an individual decision. Many writers do very well without.

If you write articles it is less important, though a well-known freelance writer may find it time-saving.

Agents are in business to make profits. They cannot afford to take on a writer about whose work they are doubtful. Once a writer is published and has shown he can repeat the process it is easier to find an agent.

It's a bargain

The agent's normal terms are an agreed percentage of earnings on work they sell (excluding Public Lending Right).

The advantage for the author is that the business side is dealt with by someone who understands it.

Action point

Start an address book of people and places, with telephone numbers, where you might find useful information.

CASE STUDIES

Yvonne finds the wrong gap

Yvonne reads several different magazines and sees that some have no stories which include children.

'I've been told to write about what I know, so I'll do a story about a little boy helping an old lady do her shopping.'

'Do you know which magazine to send it to?' her tutor asks.

'Yes,' Yvonne says confidently. 'I've found several magazines that ought to have that sort of story.'

She sends it to an upmarket glossy women's monthly. When it is rejected and she asks her tutor why, he tells her that many such magazines commissioned all their short stories, and this one is aimed at young, fashionable career women who would not be interested in children or old ladies or shopping.

Yvonne hadn't thought about the readership of the magazine and why this magazine didn't take her sort of story.

Susan should do her research

Susan reads a magazine about parentcraft. She is incensed about one article, and promptly sits down to put the other point of view, illustrating it with many anecdotes about how she has brought up her own children.

The magazine sends her article back. 'We are naturally open to all opinions,' the letter says, 'but we prefer comments on our articles in the form of short letters. We cannot run articles on the same topics for too long, and we have already had a series of articles on different theories of childcare in the past six issues.'

Susan had responded to one article without knowing the magazine policy or the background.

James studies the magazines

James plans an article on sales management. He asks the local newsagent to suggest likely magazines, and buys several to study. In one computer magazine he reads two letters complaining about shop assistants not knowing much about computers.

James goes straight to the library and asks for the last six issues of all the computer magazines they keep in stock. He spends the whole day reading them and making notes. He roughs out ideas for a long article about selling computers, and sends it to a magazine aimed at home users. It was accepted.

He had done his research, found a gap, and followed it up without wasting time or effort.

DISCUSSION POINTS

1. Make a list of all the magazines you, your family and friends read regularly. Can you persuade them to keep back copies for you so that it won't cost you money buying a lot? How can this help your market research?

2. Which categories do these magazines fall into? Can you think of ways in which you might find copies of other magazines to keep for study?

3. Think of ways to file your information about books and magazines. Would a section on particular types of magazines, or book publishers, be appropriate? Decide what information you need to collect in order to sort this information into useful categories.

4
Reading and Analysing

READING IS CRUCIAL

Have you ever thought you could write something better than the authors you read?

It is unlikely you will become a writer unless you are a voracious reader. Everything you read will have some influence on you even if you are unaware of this. You can pick up elements of style, tricks of speech, information and ideas.

Checklist

What do you read, listen to or watch, and roughly how many hours per day or week for each?

- newspapers   _____
- magazines   _____
- poetry   _____
- books — fiction   _____
- books — non-fiction   _____
- play scripts   _____
- theatre plays   _____
- radio drama   _____
- radio serials   _____
- radio documentaries   _____
- television drama   _____
- television serials   _____
- television documentaries.   _____

Action point

Do you feel the need to widen your reading? If so make a list of the types of reading you plan to tackle.

Fashions in publishing

If one publisher brings out a successful book on caring for elderly relatives others wonder whether they can get a slice of that market, and you might see a rash of similar books. The original publisher is unlikely to bring out a second one too similar though.

It's the same with drama — if a TV soap about cowboys and Indians became an overnight success there could soon be several similar soaps from rival channels.

Magazines

There are similar constraints on magazines. If you see an article comparing different types of mulch that particular magazine won't want to publish another on the same subject for some time. Send your article on mulching to a different magazine, but give it a different angle, since magazines will prefer to publish articles that take a different view of a topic rather than repeat what a rival has done.

You need to know what is being published. The only way to find out is to read.

Adapt, don't follow fashion

Any one publisher, unless he publishes category fiction, will not concentrate all his effort into one type of book. Don't send your script to the publisher who brought out the new success first.

You need to find a publisher who publishes similar types of books yet is looking for something slightly different — perhaps a modern cowboys and Indians where the Indians win, or strike oil.

If there is a new television sit-com set in a doctor's waiting room there's little chance of yours in a dentist's surgery being accepted, but a dental hospital or laboratory might just do.

ANALYSING A MAGAZINE

Short stories and articles need to be designed for particular magazines. You need to follow their style, whether light and chatty or serious and with complex arguments. The format, such as long or short paragraphs, lots of headings or none, and the length are all important. You need to know whether some themes or topics are taboo.

Look when you read

Examine magazines for the length of articles and stories. Do they always fit on one page or spread, so that readers don't have to turn over pages

COMPARING MAGAZINES

Item	Magazine A	Magazine B
no of articles/features	10	17
length	2-3 pages	1 page
variation in length	up to 50%	5-10%
is each only on one page?	no	yes
variety of topics	narrow	wide
number of words	1,500-2,000	1,000-1,200
length of paragraphs	up to 80 words	up to 40 words
length of sentences	mixed	all short
number of sections	3	7
number internal writers or editors	4	10
readers — age	25-40	50+
sex	female	male
education	advanced	basic
income	high	low
interests	fashion	sport
	jobs	entertainment
	leisure	home
	travel	puzzles

Fig. 3. Comparing two magazines.

to finish? Do the regular articles, like the cookery pages or stories of 'My life with . . .', always occupy the same space, a full page or two columns?

The lengths of sentences and paragraphs are also important. The level of difficulty, the knowledge which may be assumed, depends on the readership. You need to be aware of this too. Is the magazine for the general reader or the expert?

A technical computer magazine won't need to explain jargon like bits and bytes, roms and rams, but a teenage or parenting magazine extolling computers will. *The Times* has long sentences and paragraphs, as well as detailed explanations: *The Sun* gets to the heart of the matter in a few pithy sentences.

More than just ads
Advertisements are informative in more ways than the obvious. If you had to place ads for baby food and stair lifts which magazines would you choose? Ads tell you about readers. Use this information to send work to the right markets.

Do they have many staff writers?
In most magazines you will find a list of people such as editors and regular staff contributors. If this list is long and every aspect of the contents seems to be covered by staff writers, the magazine is less likely to accept outside freelance submissions.

Look for magazines which do not appear to have so many staff writers and depend on outside contributors.

Action point
Take three popular magazines from the same category (see Chapter 3) and analyse them for content, style, format. Make notes on every difference you can find. Figure 3 will give you an idea of how to do this.

DEVELOPING CRITICAL JUDGEMENT

Be critical
Is your reading, listening and watching purely for relaxation?

Do you make judgements or comments on what you read, such as whether it is:

- good
- clear

- well-expressed
- exciting
- interesting
- absorbing
- good of its kind
- better than other similar pieces?

Do you consciously look at the work of other writers in order to see what makes it tick, and why it is good, exciting, and so on? Apply the same techniques to your own writing.

The time spent reading is a necessary and valuable aid to writing. Use it constructively. Make notes about books or programmes. You don't need to do this all the time though it is valuable to do it in detail occasionally.

See how it's done
Cultivate a habit of mind, deliberately looking at how published writers use language and techniques.

Think about the apparently simple task of naming characters. The cast have to be individual, with appropriate names, none too similar to others. If you have Jane, June, Joan and Jean, readers will soon be confused. Who is more likely to run the corner shop — Mr Patel or Mr Cholmondeley-Majoribanks?

How does the crime writer introduce the vital clue, subtly so a careless reader does not notice, but firmly enough to avoid the charge of cheating?

How are textbooks arranged?

- What makes them appropriate for the age or level of intended readers?

- How long are the chapters and sections?

- Are there enough illustrations?

- Is the order in which difficulties are explained the best for learning or the easiest for the author?

Action point
Develop your analytical skills by studying, in one of your favourite novels, the various techniques such as:

- use of particular words
- sentence and paragraph structure
- ways of conveying information
- use of dialogue
- use of description
- ways of establishing character
- how tension is created
- use of humour
- how interest is sustained
- how pace is varied
- beginnings and endings
- what makes you want to read more.

Do the same, where appropriate, for two or more articles from contrasting magazines or newspapers, or for a play.

CONSIDERING YOUR READERS

Novels today tend to be shorter and written in a less leisurely style than they were a hundred, or even 50 years ago. People have less time to spend reading. We are also used to the rapid coverage of news and swift changes of scene on radio and television. There isn't time to dwell on the detail.

It is claimed that people's attention spans are very short, so brief scenes, fast-moving fiction, and stories and articles which can be read in a few minutes have become common.

Who will read your work?

When you know the publisher or magazine your work is being written for, you should have a good idea of the readers it will attract. For some types of writing this is more important than others.

Novels are read by people of a wide variety of ages and intellectual ability. School and college textbooks will depend on the level of knowledge or ability presumed for the age range.

Books for children have to meet both the physical and the reading ages of the children targeted. A teenager with reading problems would be insulted to be offered a book with a topic suitable for a five-year-old.

Checklist: Finding the right level

1. Do you sometimes find things too simple, or too difficult to understand?

2. Do you sometimes feel a writer is talking down to his readers?

3. Do you find writers either explain things which you think can be taken for granted, or use unexplained jargon and omit essential explanations?

Action points

1. Analyse some fiction or non-fiction to see if it is suited to its target readers.

2. For every piece of writing you do, have a picture in your mind of the age, sex, educational level, social level, and background knowledge of your ideal reader. Imagine that you are talking to this person directly as you write.

FINDING YOUR OWN VOICE

Style is individual

What is meant precisely by a writer's 'style'? Can you recognise the styles of some writers without seeing their names? Do you admire some styles more than others?

●   How would you describe the differences in style between Charles and Monica Dickens, or Anthony and Joanna Trollope?

●   How does Walter Scott differ from John Buchan and both from John le Carré?

●   Could you differentiate between scripts by Tennessee Williams, Dennis Potter, Noel Coward and Alan Ayckbourn?

●   Would you know whether a newspaper or magazine column had been written by Bernard Levin or Nigel Dempster?

What about your style?
Do you consciously imitate anyone else's style? Does your own style change depending on the topic — for example a serious argument or a flippant commentary?

Everyone has a unique writing style, a 'voice'. It may vary as a voice may be soft or angry, but it is as identifiable as a modern 'voice-print'.

Editors look for original 'voices' so don't attempt to copy the voice of someone else.

You can nevertheless learn from the styles of writers you admire, analyse how they achieve effects, and concentrate on eliminating your faults. Your style will improve and develop while remaining your own 'voice'.

Editors may have to make cuts for reasons of space but should never attempt to change a writer's style. Don't let anyone else try to either. Remember it is your work and your voice. If you allow it to be corrupted by someone else's advice, however well-intentioned, it will no longer be your work. You will not, in any case, be able to maintain a hybrid style.

Action point

Read two books (or short stories or plays) which have been written at least 50 years apart, by different authors, and make notes on how they differ in style.

You can change some things

Common 'faults' which need attention are spelling and grammatical errors, lack of clarity and repetitiveness. These can be improved by learning spelling and grammatical rules, and careful revision. Avoid clichés, too many adjectives, clumsy phrases and boring rhythms.

Aim to write **simply, clearly** and **expressively**. Good description and atmosphere can be obtained with stark, unadorned writing. One felicitous noun or verb is worth more than a string of adjectives and adverbs.

Unnecessary exposition and verbosity usually indicate a lack of confidence in your ability to express yourself clearly.

Beginners usually add when revising: professionals cut, change, and cut again. Make every word essential and the most appropriate. Verbal diarrhoea slows the action and makes the writing dull, tedious and boring.

Action point

As an exercise, take a piece of your own early prose writing and cut every superfluous word, repetition, unnecessary adverb and adjective. Aim to reduce the length by half while retaining the essential meaning. Look at every noun and see whether it is accurate. See whether a different, more expressive verb might by substituted for the one you have. Your revision will almost certainly read far more effectively than the original piece.

CASE STUDIES

Yvonne needs to read more

Yvonne works for two hours early every morning, and writes a short story a week. But they all have similar plots.

'You can explain things to children,' her tutor says. 'Why don't you look for ideas about non-fiction articles?'

Yvonne buys six well-known women's magazines and looks at them during her lunch break. She writes articles about children, teaching methods, and children's fiction. They all come back.

'You didn't research your market, you have to know the sort of topics the magazines like. You need to read lots of magazines, and several issues, before you can do that.'

'That's such a waste of time, when I ought to be writing.'

Yvonne hadn't understood that reading and analysing are important too.

Susan should know the market better

Susan thinks that if Mary can write a novel so can she. She'll try the short romances seen everywhere. She's never read any, but they are so short, they must be easy.

Susan begins the next day. After a few chapters she gets stuck, and goes out to buy several of the books. She reads them quickly, picks up several ideas, and finishes her script. After several months it is returned. It is too long and has too many characters, though the letter encourages her to keep trying. 'Have you studied our guidelines and tape?' the letter finishes.

'I didn't know about those,' Susan says. She hasn't done her research before starting.

James should know the style better

Pleased with his first success, James begins to wonder what else he knows and can use. He does a lot of gardening. Lots of magazines have gardening columns.

He studies all the 'domestic' magazines, and finds one where the gardening column is always about flowers. He sends in an article on vegetables.

The editor replies that they have a regular gardening columnist and don't accept unsolicited material.

James hasn't studied the magazines carefully enough.

DISCUSSION POINTS

1. Write brief critical notes on a few short published stories or articles. Why do you think they were published, and would any of them be suitable for expanding into longer pieces, such as a play, novel or textbook?

2. Take something simple that you know about, a mechanical device or a cookery recipe, or a process like trimming a hedge. Write down three explanations of how it works, or how to do it, for:

   - a young child
   - an adult foreigner with limited English
   - someone very like yourself.

   How and why do these explanations differ?

3. Write two letters relating some annoying event, one to a close friend, one to the local newspaper. How do they differ, and why? How might you write to the person who caused the annoyance?

CREATING A TWIST IN THE TALE

How to write successful short stories for women's magazines

Adele Ramet

For the short story writer, the twist in the tale offers excellent opportunities for publication. It is fun to write and, at 500-1200 words in length, relatively economical to produce.

This book dispels the myths and misconceptions surrounding the art of writing twist stories. It will guide you step-by-step to use characterisation, viewpoint, flashback and dialogue to maximum effect.

Adele Ramet is Chairman of the South Eastern Writers Association and an experienced creative writing tutor. She has contributed widely to *Bella, Woman's Realm*, and many other leading women's magazines.

£8.99, 128 pp illus. paperback. 1 85703 411 2.
Available from How To Books Ltd, Plymbridge House, Estover Road, Plymouth PL6 7PZ.
Customer Services Tel: (01752) 202301. Fax: (01752) 202331.
Please add postage & packing (£1 UK, £2 Europe, £3 world airmail).
Credit card orders may be faxed or phoned.

5
Getting Ideas

WHERE TO FIND IDEAS

There are various sources of ideas and writers can use all of them.

Ideas alone are not enough

One of the first questions non-writers ask is 'Where do you get all your ideas?' Often a writer's problem is not too few, but too many ideas. Ideas alone won't make a writer, they have to be organised, put together, described, and developed.

They'll come if you work at it

A friend once said 'Inspiration is a blank sheet of paper'. You don't write unless you sit down ready to do it, even if there are no ideas in your head to begin with.

Action points

1. Write down the titles of books, songs or films, and see if they spark off other ideas.

2. Write down three things which have annoyed you, or made you happy, or three random objects, and try to construct a plot or an article from what you put down.

3. Make notes about possible characters, even if you haven't yet got a story to put them into.

4. Make lists of names you could use. One might suggest a story, but the lists will be useful. One of the dangers authors find is using the same name again, when too lazy to find a new one.

5. Write descriptions of places or scenery, journeys or events, food and restaurants, and so on, ready for the time you may want something of that kind.

These methods help
It won't always work, but you have more chance of a story or article developing when you have something tangible to look at.

You can search for ideas anywhere
You can do a lot during your day-to-day life to get ideas:

● Observe people round you and try to memorise how they look, then write it down later as the basis for your own characters.

● Eavesdrop on conversations, listening to how people phrase things.

● Listen for odd remarks which could give ideas for a plot or the title of a story.

Use your reading to suggest ideas

● Look at myths and fairy stories and relate them to modern life.

● Stand situations on their head.

● Use your own personal experience or that of others.

● Look for ideas in places, people, history, geography, famous titles or quotations.

● Newspaper stories and advertisements can provide the starting point.

● An unusual murder can prompt a novel or a play, an article on crime prevention, a series on other strange murders, and many more.

● An advertisement for 'selling an old friend' could be a car, pony, husband or computer — what a story that could make.

● Look for ideas in agony columns and letters.

● Guide books and anthologies can spark off ideas for both fiction and non-fiction.

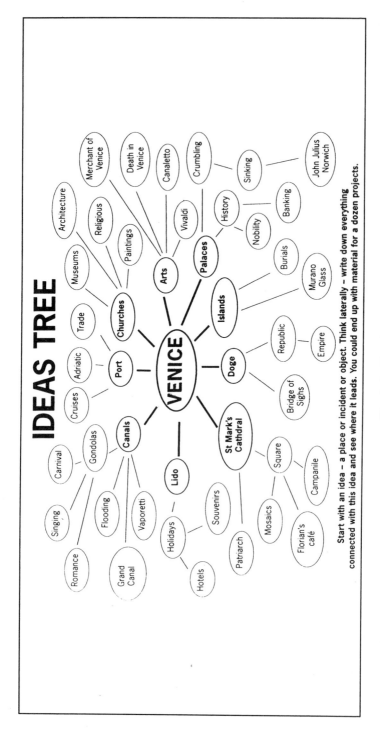

Fig. 4. An ideas tree.

Action point
Create an ideas tree for yourself, starting with something you are familiar with (see Figure 4).

ASKING QUESTIONS

Inspiration on its own is not often productive. You have to create ideas
from what you see or hear. **Ask who, what, when, where, how, why
and what if?**

For example you see an isolated house. To many people it would be
just that. A fiction writer would instantly ask:

- Who lives there?
- Why?
- Why do they choose seclusion?
- When did they go there?
- Where did they come from?
- How did they find it?
- What if they are invaded by . . . (A romantic novelist will suppose
  a hero, a crime writer a villain, a sci-fi addict aliens from space.)

An article writer will think of:

- a series on isolated houses
- odd living quarters
- planning permission
- turning it into an hotel or golf club.

Action points

1. Make a list of the ways in which you will look for ideas.

2. Make a list of some ideas you could use.

TAKING A FRESH APPROACH

Give the story a twist
Take a well known real story and retell it from the point of view of a
minor character — Red Riding Hood's woodcutter, perhaps.

Bring it up to date. Make it a crime story or one where Red Riding
Hood is taken into care by social services.

Ask what would have happened if Dick Whittington hadn't reached London.

Tell Cinderella's life if she'd stayed too long at the ball.

What might have happened if Romeo's and Juliet's families had agreed to their marriage?

You will not use these exact characters and names, but think of a similar or parallel situation.

There are articles everywhere

Almost every news report can prompt an article idea. If there is a serious road accident you could do articles on:

- previous accidents in the vicinity

- traffic problems and a survey on how these have been tackled elsewhere

- the lives of people in the emergency services

- what would happen with a similar but major disaster

- previous victims and how the accidents changed their lives, or the lives of their families

- insurance

- compensation.

Action point

Look at today's newspaper, select three reports of different kinds of events, and make lists of possible articles arising from them.

LOOKING BEHIND THE FACTS

Statistics are real people

Social surveys are fertile sources of ideas. If you see figures for how many households have televisions and refrigerators, look at the ones which don't. Try to find some, and explain how they manage without.

USING YOUR IMAGINATION

This is not a matter of inventing people and incidents, but of being able to see how they can be used in new and exciting ways. Non-fiction writers also need imagination to find new angles or a fresh approach.

It may not be totally true to claim there is nothing new under the sun, since there are always new inventions. These are often the product of a scientist's imagination and asking questions.

The old and familiar can be viewed from a different perspective and thus provide enlightenment. Think of the puzzle pictures of commonplace objects and how different and strange they appear when photographed from below or foreshortened, or at an unusual magnification. The writer can do similar things.

Keep it under control

It is useful for a writer to have imagination, but it has to be directed and controlled.

It isn't a story if a space traveller simply goes on a long journey and meets lots of fascinating aliens and weird communities or landscapes. There has to be a purpose.

Similarly an article must have a shape, a structure, to make it publishable. An account of a walk through a village, describing every building seen, will be rather pointless. An article about the history of the village, or featuring some of the buildings, perhaps those of architectural interest, or those built during a certain century, is selective and allows for comparisons, giving it a focus.

CASE STUDIES

Yvonne covers the same ground

Yvonne wants to write a book about farm animals. She looks at similar books and takes one of them as her guide.

She knows she mustn't copy directly, that is plagiarism, but she follows the same pattern of a chapter for each animal. She tells how they are looked after, what they eat, and what food they produce. She sends it to a publisher who hasn't done a book on farm animals, and is disappointed when her script comes back.

Some time later that publisher publishes a book on farm animals, and Yvonne buys it, feeling angry. This book tells the story of how each animal has become domesticated, or been brought to England, which other parts of the world also have these animals, and how they are different in other countries.

Yvonne's script has been the same old thing again, but this one is inventive and different.

Susan's ideas run away

Susan gets carried away with her romance. As well as the love story she
has Arab spies, a bank robbery, the murder of a small child, the rape of
a young girl, several car chases and one character who conducts seances
and can send people on time travels.

The love story becomes bogged down in all the other distractions,
and by the time Susan has written a hundred pages she has barely started
the main story.

Susan has plenty of ideas, but is undisciplined in using them.

James gets an idea from an agony column

James is waiting for his wife to finish shopping and begins to read the
advice page in one of her magazines.

A widow couldn't cope with a large garden but didn't want to move
house. James knows how much gardens mean to people. He writes an
article about ways people might cope. He suggests labour-saving plants,
wildlife habitats, and sharing the produce with a flat-dweller. After some
research he sends it to one of the retirement magazines.

The article is accepted, and James begins to look in places such as
letters and news reports for ideas.

DISCUSSION POINTS

1. Explain where most of your ideas come from.

2. What other sources of ideas do you think might be useful for you?

3. Using either the Venice Ideas Tree (see Figure 4) or your own, make
    lists of all the articles or stories that could be written from each of
    the words highlighted. They don't have to be subjects you are
    already an expert on. How many have you thought of, and of those
    how many might you actually attempt to write?

6
Developing Ideas

EXPANDING YOUR IDEAS

Stories and articles can arise from odd snippets which form the basis of a plot or idea, or can be planned deliberately by calculating what is currently popular and devising work from this.

Find a new angle

The technique of compiling a story or an article out of a few ordinary facts is one which can be learned. However mundane a situation appears on the surface, ask questions such as those in Chapter 5. You will begin to see ways of developing it in an original and interesting manner for possible publication.

Explore behind the scenes

Be aware of the history and geography of places you know or visit. They don't have to be exotic foreign locations — readers are becoming more interested in local history. Use them as backgrounds for stories or starting points for factual articles — or one on the growth of local history societies and how to run these.

Look beyond the obvious

Look out for unusual couples, unlikely companions, and look at reasons for them to be together. This could suggest a story or an article on unusual marriages, by age or culture or religion.

Be aware of alternatives

Take famous titles and think how they could be used for totally different types of stories. *Three Men in a Boat* could be a modern smuggling story, or an article on the prevention of smuggling. *Calamity Jane* might be a romance about an inept secretary or an article on efficient office management.

Action points

1. Make up a story with three separate characters in a special situation. For example an old man, a young woman, and a child in a supermarket.

2. Think up a magazine article which is not simply a news item, on a topical issue such as conservation or the state of British sport.

3. Think of a new angle for either of the above. For example the child is the old man's son, or the state of sport is due to the British weather.

KEEPING TRACK OF IDEAS

On the tip on my tongue
One of the most frustrating things is to have a brilliant idea in the middle of the night only to forget it by the time you get up. Witty snatches of conversation can be taking place in your head but vanish before you can capture them in your story. The perfect way of developing your argument in a complicated article is lost beyond recall, and the name of a new magazine or a sympathetic editor looking for material is just on the tip of your tongue.

Write them down
Few writers are fortunate enough to possess total recall of ideas they once had, so it is important to write them down. Always have a pen and paper with you beside the bed, in the kitchen, in your pocket or bag, and write down ideas or notes as they occur.

So long as you don't throw away the old envelope and do collect up all the notes lying in different places about the house you will have lots of new ideas and solutions to work on.

Action point
Make sure you provide paper and pen in all the places where they could be useful.

ORGANISING IDEAS

Perhaps the next scene will just not come, you cannot get past a particular snag, you don't know how to wind up some argument or draw together all the strands. The more you puzzle at it the worse it seems until you are tempted to throw away the whole idea.

When to forget it

If you are stuck forget it for a while. Do something else. This can be a different piece of writing or a quite distinct activity. Usually the solution will emerge from your subconscious, and so long as you have pen and paper at the ready you can note it for use next time you come to your desk.

Of course sometimes the solution will not come, and then you have to examine the problem in more detail to see whether in fact there is no satisfactory answer. If so you may have to abandon the project or turn it round so a solution can be found.

FILING YOUR IDEAS

Often an idea for a character or a situation may occur while you are writing one novel or play but cannot be used in it.

Similarly ideas for different articles come at inappropriate times. Because magazines go to press weeks or months before the actual publication date, it would be pointless sending in an article about Easter on Good Friday. You may, however, be able to use it later in the year and submit it in plenty of time for next Easter.

The most organised writers will have file cards or computer files in which to store ideas. Some will use loose-leaf books, and pocket-sized loose-leaf diaries and notebooks are ideal for writers. You can jot down ideas as they come, on different pages, perhaps using different coloured pages for different things, and file them later.

At the very least designate one desk drawer or a box file or an envelope file as your ideas depository. You may not want to have a full-blown filing system, perhaps because you think you don't have many ideas or because you don't yet know what method would be the most helpful, what sections and sub-sections to have.

Checklist: How do you keep and organise ideas?

- in your head
- scraps of paper everywhere
- scraps of paper in one file or drawer
- notebooks
- file cards
- loose-leaf files
- computer files.

Action points

1. Decide how you will organise your collection of ideas.

2. Periodically look through your notes in search of ideas for extending your existing project or beginning new ones.

REVISING YOUR IDEAS

It is possible to spend all your time doing the organising rather than getting on with the writing. But if you get into the habit of writing down your ideas you will be pleasantly surprised to see how many you have collected over the course of a month.

When you need a new idea, are looking for inspiration, or when you already have an idea for an article and you know you have various relevant notes somewhere, or can't settle to composing, go through the drawer and sort.

Even if you find no new idea at least your notes will be in a better order, and you will be reminded of past ideas which might germinate in your subconscious ready for tomorrow or next week.

CASE STUDIES

Yvonne works on her notes

Yvonne files her notes and her research carefully, and can always find whatever she wants. One day she realises how many she's gathered to do with teaching.

'What can I do with all this?' she asks her tutor.

'You could write a huge book but be selective. Choose three sheets at random and see if that gives you any ideas.'

Yvonne thinks this is odd advice but she picks out a note about the national curriculum paperwork, another about a dyslexic child, and one on a reading system based on colours.

She devises a colour-coded chart for making it easier to assess children for different aspects, and writes an article about it. She sells it to an educational magazine.

Susan pins her hopes on word processing

Susan buys herself a word processor. It will help her to keep track of her story. The salesman tries to persuade her to go on a study-course, but she says she can learn it from the manual.

Susan spends one evening learning the basic techniques. She will start tomorrow when the house is empty.

'Can I play a game on it?' her son asks next evening.

'When you've done your homework. Gosh, I'm tired.'

Susan switches off the machine. 'I'll get tea now.'

'Did you save it first?' her son asks. 'If you didn't, you'll have lost it.'

Susan is too impatient and hasn't understood she has to save what she's typed. She has all the work to do again.

James gets organised

James is accumulating vast quantities of notes, often duplicating them, and no good ideas of how to organise them.

'Couldn't your computer help?' his wife asks.

'If I put them on a computer it would be easier to find them,' he agrees.

James spends several days sorting out his notes and putting them into the computer files. 'This is so much easier,' he says.

'It saves space too,' she says. 'Can we get rid of some of these old papers?'

James nods. 'But wait until I've made a back-up copy in case I lose the stuff on the computer.'

James has taken his time to find out which system is best for him, and has organised his notes so that he can find them easily.

DISCUSSION POINTS

1. Are you making your notes in the most useful way? Would it help if you were to be more methodical, such as always using the same size of paper, or dating and heading them? Think of ways to make your life easier.

2. How much do you know about computers and word processors? Consider seriously how you might use one, or if you already have one, use it more fully.

3. Stories and articles can develop in many different directions. If you start with two characters, or a controversial statement, how many different situations can you think of that might arise?

7
The All-Important Beginnings

PLANNING A PROJECT

Where to start

There are several important steps when setting out to write a story or article:

- making the idea original and interesting

- having the right market in mind

- knowing the style and length you intend to write

- knowing what research you need to do, and where to do it.

The detailed planning

Make notes

This helps you to arrange your ideas, plan a timetable, and remind yourself of what you need to do.

These notes can be scrappy phrases, so long as you understand them, or a very detailed outline which only needs to be expanded to form the basis of the article or book.

Deadlines help

It's a good idea to set yourself a deadline. Within that time limit plan how long you will need for the physical writing, and how much time you may need for the research. If it is a long project like a book, break it down into sections and decide how long it will take you to do each section.

An example

Let us suppose you want to write a profile about a local celebrity, for the local newspaper. The article may be 1,000 words long, an amount which can be written in a morning. It is probable, however, that you will need much longer for considering and arranging your material, perhaps two full days or the equivalent. You will collect far more information than you can use and will need to be very selective.

You will need to interview the subject of your article, and celebrities are usually busy people. It may be some time before your subject can find time for the interview.

You will need some background information before you do the interview. This might be reading things your subject has written, or perhaps biographies of them, or cuttings from the local and national press. It could take weeks for the libraries to obtain the books you want, and several visits to libraries or newspaper offices to consult their files. You may need to talk to other people, and this could involve travelling to visit them.

A short article could take weeks to set up and research. Of course you will be doing other things in the meantime, but it would be over-optimistic to promise the article for next week unless you are certain you already have all the details and facilities you need.

Most articles do not require nearly so much preparation, but you need to be aware of what is involved. Then you are neither overwhelmed nor depressed when extra work is shown to be necessary.

The timetable is a guide
It may not always be possible to keep to your preliminary timetable. Don't despair. With experience you will come to know the practicalities and set yourself realistic targets. When you have done this it is satisfying to know you are up to date, and even better if you finish early and have time to do something extra.

THE FIRST WORDS ARE VITAL

The most important step towards starting is to sit at your desk and pick up your pen.

Overcoming procrastination
Procrastination, the 'clear the desk first' syndrome, is a peril for almost every writer, however experienced or successful. It will probably attack you. It doesn't mean you can't or don't want to write. Once started a real writer will be anxious to carry on and finish. However, if you procrastinate too much ask yourself seriously whether you do truly want to write, or whether you are trying to write the wrong things.

What to write

Having got to the stage of setting pen to paper remember that your first sentence, or paragraph, is the most important one of all.

HOOKING THE READER

You have to give the reader a reason for continuing.

The first few words make readers carry on because:

● they set the tone

● they convey the impression the work will be interesting, intriguing, exciting, informative, controversial, or boring.

If it is boring the reader will abandon the effort. A good editor will read further in the hope that the work is publishable, knowing that beginnings often need changing.

Articles have to grab readers within seconds
Most readers skim through a newspaper or magazine deciding what to read now and what they might read when they have time — time which rarely materialises.

Start with something challenging, debatable, curious, startling, or outrageous (see Figure 5).

Radio drama is different
The listener has to become accustomed to the voices of the actors, so having a crucial sentence right at the start is not a good idea. Except on tape it cannot be re-heard, as writing can be re-read. However, it must be interesting enough to make the audience keep listening.

WRITING A BEGINNING AT THE END

Beginnings are vital but too many writers spend so much time polishing that first sentence or chapter they never move on. You also have to finish things.

If you cannot think of the ideal beginning, carry on. Probably something later on in the work will give you a brilliant idea for how to start. Many novelists do only a rough draft of their first chapters and rewrite them when the rest of the book is finished.

SOME ARRESTING BEGINNINGS

Anita Burgh, *The Azure Bowl* (Chatto and Windus 1989)

Alice Tregowan's upbringing had been unconventional. Her mother, Etty, hated her. George, her father, seemed unaware of her existence.

Norma Curtis, *Living It Up, Living It Down* (HarperCollins 1995)

As hostess, Catrin Howden didn't actually mind her guests playing Russian Roulette — it was just the thought of the mess it made on the towels.

Marika Cobbold, *Guppies For Tea* (Black Swan Books (Transworld Publishers) 1993)

'And there's the Admiral.' Sister Morris gave a cheery wave into the gloom of the residents' lounge. 'We like to sit him by the aquarium; reminds him of his seafaring days, I always think.'

Eleanor Rees, *The Seal Wife* (Mills and Boon 1989)

Adam Dale did not seduce his housekeepers. Nor did he beat them, drink their wages, or expect them to sleep in a scarcely converted, unheated hayloft. From all these points of view he was a model employer. So why was it that not one of the three women Cathy had selected had lasted more than a month?

Fig. 5. Hooking your reader from the outset.

Checklist: Start at the beginning

1. Do you spend a lot of time polishing and rewriting the beginning?

2. Do you feel you have to get the beginning perfect before you can move on?

3. Do you look at the beginning sentences and paragraphs of other, especially popular work?

4. Do you analyse the beginnings of published pieces you read?

Action point
Read the beginning paragraphs of ten novels/short stories/articles/other every week, and decide which of them you would like to finish reading, and why.

STARTING TOO SOON

Starting your story at the right time
Many fiction writers start at a point which is too early with a résumé of the main character's life so far. You need action, not reflection.

Use an exciting event or period in a character's life and slip in just the essential background, later on, to explain that, for example, the heroine is wary of dogs because she was bitten as a child.

Novices also try to convey too much information too soon. This can be boring and unproductive if the reader has forgotten a fact when it becomes important.

This applies to articles as well — too much background at the beginning is not necessary and will probably turn the reader off before they reach the point of the piece.

CHOOSING THE RIGHT TITLE

Be brief. Long titles take up too much space. Some writers always start with the title. Others never find one until the piece is finished.

Magazines and newspapers choose their own headlines to fit their style and the space available.

No copyright
Titles will be repeated, especially with articles. This doesn't matter,

there is no copyright in titles, but entitling your play *Hamlet* wouldn't be a good idea. Editors like originality.

They attract attention
Titles capture the editor's and reader's attention and say something about the work. Which would you prefer: *Ten Recipes for Using Minced Meat* or *Let's Mince Matters?*

Where to find them
Many titles depend on alliteration. Play with words until you find a good combination. Suppose you have a struggle in Coventry. Write down synonyms for 'struggle'. Look in *Roget's Thesaurus* or a dictionary of synonyms for inspiration. *Coventry Conflict* might suit, or forget the town and choose *The Battle Boys*.

You can use puns, phrases from poetry, quotations or straightforward descriptive phrases or words. Your choice must be appropriate for your style and potential readers. *A Life of Bach* would be more suitable for a biography than *Bach's Bark*.

Checklist: How are you on titles?

1. Can you think of titles easily?

2. Do you often find titles of books you read inappropriate or misleading?

3. Do you ever try to devise different titles for books you read?

4. If you were stuck for a title how would you set about finding one?

Action points

1. Devise alternative titles for the next few books or magazine articles you read.

2. In your files begin a section for titles you might one day use.

CASE STUDIES

Yvonne tries too hard
Yvonne thinks she can do another article about colour coded filing sys-

tems, organising recipes. She aims to sell it to a glossy monthly magazine which has a big cookery section.

She knows how important the start is, but she can't think just how to catch the readers' attention. After several days of dithering she has a few ideas, none of them exciting. She spends hours revising and polishing the first few paragraphs.

She begins to think it isn't worth it. She will never get to the end if it all takes so long.

Yvonne is losing interest in the whole project.

Susan starts her story too soon

Susan abandons her first novel when it becomes too complicated to finish. She starts another, with just four main characters.

To make it simple, she introduces one new character in each chapter, giving the reader their background. This way it will be easy to manage.

'You start quite well,' Mary says when Susan shows her the first few chapters. 'But you start too soon'.

'Readers need to know about them,' Susan answers.

'Yes, but not all this. Most of this information can be slipped in later, when it's appropriate and will explain to the reader what is happening.'

Susan should start later in the story.

James spends time analysing

James often can't find the right beginnings. He decides to see how successful writers do it. He looks at some novels, and goes through his magazines, reading just the first paragraphs.

'I'm beginning to see why a few of them make me want to carry on, and why I never read these other articles at the time.'

His wife looks at his books. 'They are different from those Victorian novels we read at school,' she says.

James agrees. 'Fashions change. They could afford long descriptions then. People want to get on with it now.'

James has used his reading time constructively, and knows how to catch the reader's attention.

DISCUSSION POINTS

1. Are you keeping your lists of useful addresses and contacts up to date? Have you new ideas by now of other, perhaps better ways of organising these lists?

2. Make a list of the things you feel you have to do before you sit down to write. Is this procrastination, and how can you avoid it?

3. Have you had brilliant ideas for the beginning sentences of books or articles? You can write them down and keep for further use. How would you file them?

8
Middles and Ends

Beginnings and ends are crucial, but it's the middles that separate good writers from average ones.

While the beginning will attract a reader, it's the satisfying end that will make him come back for more.

The middle, during which the reader's interest has to be maintained, is often the most difficult.

WORKING TO THE RIGHT LENGTH

Why length matters

Many magazines are designed so that each week or month the short stories or the cookery pages occupy the same amount of space. It is the production editor's or sub-editor's job to make sure the piece fits, and if the wordage is accurate this task is much easier.

Some adjustments can be made by using larger or smaller pictures, or more sub-headings, but cutting a piece by half and still keeping its character is difficult.

Category novels, such as those by Harlequin Mills and Boon, often have the same number of pages. This makes costing simpler for the publisher, and the books have the same look, sold by the reputation of the product. In these books more can be done by changing the type size or page layout to fit variations in length, but authors should still aim to write within five to ten per cent either side of the suggested length.

Radio and TV plays and talks have to fit the required time. Minor adjustments can be made when recording, but the actors cannot simply speed up to get through the script in the way weather forecasters sometimes do.

How to count words
You don't need to count every one
Occasionally writers have painstakingly counted every word. This isn't

necessary, the nearest thousand (for a novel) and hundred (for a short story or article) is enough.

With computer word counts many people put the exact number of words their machines calculate, but there are traps in this method:

- The computer cannot always omit from the total things like your name and the title on each page.

- An academic treatise with many long words will occupy more space than a simple reading book for young children.

- A book with lots of dialogue in short speeches will occupy more lines than one with long unbroken paragraphs.

- A book with many short chapters will occupy more pages than one with a few very long chapters.

- A book with tables and diagrams and lists will take up more space than one without.

- The same principles apply to articles and short stories.

White space has to be counted too
This means the spaces at the beginnings and ends of short lines and chapters. A publisher needs to know this to work out how many pages the book will occupy, and therefore how much it will cost to print.

A magazine editor is even more restricted for space. See Figure 6 for an example of how to calculate wordage.

Action point
Take a typical piece of your writing and calculate the number of words per page.

KEEPING UP THE INTEREST

Know where you're going
Do you sometimes abandon reading something half way through? If so, why?

Do you sometimes feel your project is becoming a chore? Do you sometimes cut the length from what you planned because it seems too long?

The recommended method is to count the words in ten full lines of typescript or longhand. Note them in the margin as below.

<pre>
     WHAT EDITORS DO
     Book publishing
11   The book editor will buy your work, guide you through the
 8   necessary changes, oversee the process of publication, and
     be your main contact.
          Revision doesn't stop on acceptance. A book is edited
10   for content, changes and errors, then copy-edited for house
10   style and consistency. With novels an editor may ask for
 9   sections to be rewritten, suggest some characters be removed
 9   or made less important, others be given greater prominence.
10   The writer may be asked to emphasise particular scenes, do
     them in a different way, and other changes.
          Illustrations may be needed. It is then typeset. The
 9   cover will be planned, publication date set, and publicity
 6   schedules organised, including advertising campaigns and
     sales promotions.
          After typesetting proofs have to be checked and
 8   alterations made. Second rights are negotiated and review
     copies sent out. The author may be involved in promotional
     interviews, book signings, or giving talks.

     Magazines
     In magazines, articles must be edited to fit available
     spaces, artists commissioned and illustrations incorporated.
     Often editorial content is planned to fit in with special
     advertising campaigns or shows and exhibitions.
          Some editing, sub-editing and cutting on magazines is
     done when the pages are laid out.
                         * * * * *
</pre>

Adding them up comes to 90 words. Divide by ten to get the average number per line:

$$\frac{90}{10} = 9$$

Then add up the number of lines per full page of script, let's say 30. Multiply by the average number of words per line:

$$\begin{array}{r} 30 \\ 9 \times \\ \hline 270 \end{array}$$

to give you an average number of words per page of 270. Multiply this figure by the total number of pages and you have a good enough approximation of your total length.

If your typescript for an article is four pages long, 270 x 4 = 1,080 words. Approximately 1,100 is good enough.

If your novel typescript is 415 pages long, 270 x 415 = 112,050 words. 112,000 is near enough.

Fig. 6. How to calculate words.

Fiction

In a novel the situation is set up, the characters introduced, the theme and the conflict are in place. The author must carry on with the story, maintaining the suspense, weaving in all the strands, most of all carrying the reader along.

Throughout a novel there must be changes of pace. Aim for alternating peaks of activity and excitement with troughs for reflection and explanation. A novel where nothing much happens and the pace is monotonous is boring. A story lurching from one crisis to the next without pause is equally bad, it leaves the reader surfeited.

If the main peak comes too soon what follows can seem pale. It is not enough to contrive more and more incidents to fill the allotted pages. They must lead somewhere, show development of plot or character.

Short stories and drama have similar structures though the complications and characters are fewer.

Non-fiction

In non-fiction argument and exposition come in the middle. This must be carefully devised in a logical order, and where appropriate follow on from a previous section, graduated for difficulty if necessary.

Sometimes it is very straightforward such as 'Here are ten ways of staying slim' — the middle describes each in turn — concluding with good wishes for a slimmer, healthier future.

In textbooks, the beginning will survey the ground to be covered, perhaps summarising what should already be known. There will be carefully graded chapters with exercises, each resting on the knowledge conveyed previously and using only terms and concepts already explained. The end will be a résumé of what has been learned.

Action point

Analyse a book or article you have given up reading part way through and find out why you did not want to continue.

AVOIDING WRITER'S BLOCK

Checklist: What stops you writing?

1.   Are there times when you cannot think what to write next?

2.   Do you sometimes decide that what you have written is rubbish?

3. Do you get to the middle of a story and then cannot think of a satisfactory ending?

4. Do you start a piece and not know how to finish it?

Solving the problem

There is nothing unusual about being unable to carry on with a piece of work. It happens to all writers at some time. Occasionally the solution has to be to scrap the work, decide that it wasn't a good idea and would not have worked.

This is disappointing but not a complete waste of time. You will have learned something in the process, if only not to bother with that type of project again.

How you overcome the problem of not knowing how to go on depends on the type and length of the work.

If it is a novel the ending must flow from what your characters are and what they have done. Reread the novel and you may see how it should end or how you could change earlier parts or characters to lead up to a conclusion.

With an article it is often simpler to keep the whole shape in your head from the beginning. Select just a few ideas to convey, and the problem of not knowing how to end is less likely to occur.

Look to see whether you have tried to cover too much. Perhaps you have included too many disparate ideas so that a tidy summing up is not possible. Sometimes the only possible conclusion is 'we'll have to see what happens in the future'. But don't use this too often; in most articles it is possible to come to some sort of conclusion.

It will come

If you don't discover a solution straight away put the work aside for a few days or weeks and do something else. The solution may emerge and you will not have wasted too much time agonising over it.

The something else could be:

● writing or planning another project

● doing research

● going through your ideas file either in search of a new idea or to organise it

- writing anything

- missing this section and going to another

- starting a different project

- having a cup of coffee

- going for a walk

- writing a letter to a friend

- doing something so boring that writing will appear an escape from it.

GETTING THE ENDING RIGHT

How often do you finish a book or article and wish it was twice as long? How often do you find endings unsatisfactory? What are the reasons for this? Do you sometimes feel the ending has been cut short or prolonged too much?

Action point
Analyse the endings of the next ten books, articles or plays you read and write down how they have been constructed.

Wrap it up
Any work has to be tied up in an adequate way. This does not necessarily mean every strand is neatly tucked in. Sometimes it is more effective for the reader to be able to imagine an outcome that the writer leaves unwritten.

In a crime novel, however, it would frustrate the reader if it were not explained how the solution was arrived at. An article will usually summarise the points or arguments in order to draw a conclusion or highlight the most important.

Writers can rush to finish, thankful to be reaching the end of a project. In the haste essential explanations can be overlooked or a scene dealt with in too summary a fashion for the reader's satisfaction.

As much care must be taken with the ending as with the beginning. If necessary it must be revised or rewritten until it is as good as the writer can manage.

Have you ever asked yourself why books such as *Gone with the Wind* and *Rebecca* were so successful, and new authors are commissioned to write sequels? They are love stories like many other books but look at the endings. To many readers they are unsatisfactory — they were looking for a happy ending and the author did not oblige. Hence the massive sales and film deals for sequels before they are even written.

CASE STUDIES

Yvonne needs to re-think

There is an argument in the media about the amount of work teachers have to do. Yvonne keeps a work diary and writes an article to show how long everything takes her. This time she finds a good opening, but when she shows it to her tutor he shakes his head.

'You have to keep the reader's interest,' he tells her.

'I do. I mention every single thing I do, from preparing lessons the night before to fastening up shoes when the children go home, and then the endless paperwork and staff meetings.'

'That's just it, you simply make a list, there's no tension or development.'

Yvonne hasn't considered the need to entice her readers to continue.

Susan finishes too quickly

Susan has written 60,000 words. Her hero and heroine have overcome most of their problems and in the last chapter the final misunderstanding is resolved when a friend confesses to a trick.

'Thank goodness,' she says. 'Now I can wrap it up.'

The lovers meet outside the hero's house on the last page, smile and kiss. The end.

'But that's not satisfying,' Mary says. 'The reader wants more, an explanation, and a more prolonged reconciliation. This way it's like glimpsing a feast and having it taken away before you even start to nibble.'

Susan is so impatient to finish that she skimps the ending.

James takes a break

James is writing what he hopes will be a humorous article on the trials of DIY. It starts well with a ludicrous incident, goes on to relate various other amusing experiences, but he just can't think of a satisfying way to end it.

He decides to forget writing and take his grandchildren for a day out at the local safari park.

Idly watching the keepers in their tower in the lion enclosure, he wonders what would happen if the structure collapsed because of bad workmanship, or even ants eating away the base.

'That's it!' he exclaims. 'I can end on an absurd note.'

James has banished writer's block by forgetting his problem for a while.

DISCUSSION POINTS

1. Do you normally write more words or fewer than you intend? Can you analyse why, and decide what to do about it?

2. When and why do you get writer's block? Are there different ways of working, or different forms of writing you might try, in order to overcome it?

3. Are your endings too drawn out or too abrupt? Can you find ways of making your endings satisfy you and your readers?

9
Editing Your Work

First drafts, revision and polishing projects are all essential if you are to be successful.

REWRITING

Some writers hate the chore of revising. Other would-be writers never seem to finish anything, but may have drawers full of notes. Some enjoy revising more than creating the original draft.

Checklist: Starting, polishing, and ending
What is most important to you?

- getting something down quickly
- starting new projects
- polishing and revising your work
- finishing a project.

If you rarely finish a project have you asked yourself why?

Action point
Sort out all your unfinished projects and divide them into piles:

- those you could throw away

- those you could finish in the way you originally intended

- those you might adapt, either by doing them differently or incorporating into wider projects or splitting into two or more separate projects

- those which only need revision to make them potentially saleable.

Complete the piece first

Complete the first draft quickly, however roughly. Don't try to do too much detailed revision until you have this, completed in that it has reached the end of the story or what you have to say in an article. There is the danger of spending so much time on the opening that you never get to the end.

Rewriting does not mean sitting down and doing the same article again, but differently. This would not be very constructive. It would be the same as another first draft. The same errors would probably creep in while some of the spontaneity, the original first flush of enthusiasm, would be lost.

Rewriting means going over the piece of work to:

- check for errors
- decide whether certain things might be expressed more clearly
- put points in a different order.

In fiction it might mean:

- adding or removing a scene
- adding or removing a character, strand or sub-plot
- changing a scene to dialogue instead of narrative
- writing a scene in a different way
- putting scenes in a different order
- rewriting a section from another character's viewpoint.

Action point

Take an old piece of work and revise it bearing in mind the above points. Figure 7 shows how and why a piece can be corrected.

WHAT TO LOOK FOR

When you are rewriting you are effectively editing your work. Editing and sub-editing can mean simply checking for typing errors but ought to be far more.

In all your work

- check spellings, in particular consistency
- check grammar

AUTHOR'S CHANGES TO FIRST DRAFT
WITH EXPLANATIONS

PROOFREADING

By ~~the time you get to the~~ proofreading stage all the ~~corrections~~ ~~of both the~~ edit*ing* and the author's ~~will~~ have be~~en~~ done. It ~~is~~ expensive ~~to make changes afterwards~~. ~~If you write books~~ You *probably* may be asked to read the proof*s of books*, but ~~this will~~ not happen with ma*g*azine pieces.

~~When~~ A professional proofreader ~~reads the piece she/he~~ will read the work ~~several~~ *two or three* times, looking for ~~lots of many~~ different things. T*he first* ~~begin with~~ read *is* for sense, ~~but~~ ~~some~~ errors, words or phrases missed, are picked up ~~at this stage~~. The second read concentrates on punctuation ~~and words~~, comparing ~~the~~ proofs with ~~the~~ original, checking inconsistencies, spellings, and ~~corrections the editor might have made~~ *editor's* *comments better*.

Publishers can interpret ~~your suggestions~~ *comments better* if you use *standard* proofreading symbols. These are found in *handbooks* ~~and~~ some dictionaries. You will need only a dozen symbols, but is it ~~valuable to~~ *worth* know*ing* them – it adds to the professional image.

1	brisker start
2	briefer and better order
3	same topic, no new paragraph
4	shorter
5	more exact
6	more succinct
7	typo
8	saves repeat
9	no need both
10	more precise
11	keep in same sentence
12	superfluous words
13	repeat
14	better order words more important
15	unnecessary
16	better order
17	shorter
18	better word
19	comparison
20	makes clearer

21 more accurate	22 symbols are in handbooks, so mention
23 more accurate	24 alter emphasis

Fig. 7. A sample of corrected work.

PROOFREADING — FINAL VERSION
AFTER CORRECTIONS

By proofreading stage editing and author's corrections
should be done. Later changes are expensive. You will
probably be asked to read proofs of books, but not magazine
pieces.

A professional proofreader will read work two or three
times, looking for different things.

The first read is for sense but some errors, words or
phrases missed, are picked up. The second concentrates on
words and punctuation, comparing proofs with original,
checking spellings, inconsistencies and editor's
corrections.

Publishers can interpret your comments better if you
use standard proofreading symbols. These are in handbooks
and some dictionaries. You probably need only a dozen
symbols, but it is worth knowing these - it adds to the
professional image.

Fig. 8. The corrected version.

79

- check that the meaning is always clear
- if you overuse the same word or expression try to find synonyms
- cut superfluous words and sentences
- make sure paragraphing is appropriate
- eliminate clichés.

In articles and non-fiction books:

- make sure there is a logical sequence to your arguments

- double check facts and quotations

- make sure you know where all the facts come from

- keep a list of references in case you need to refer to them again or provide proof

- check and double check that facts are true and fair — not juicy but insubstantial gossip or a malicious and irrelevant statement

- publishers will normally check too, but it is also the writer's responsibility to ensure against libel.

In fiction:

- ensure your characters do not change name or appearance midway

- make them speak appropriately, using dialect or special speech patterns consistently

- make their behaviour consistent with their characters or motivations

- use description accurately, especially of places

- check that daffodils are not blooming in autumn

- check that journeys can be completed in the time allowed

- check that you do not have ten days in a week

- if you are being very specific as to time or place check factual aspects such as train timetables or routes, weather conditions and pub opening times.

Make it perfect

When you find something wrong or less than perfect correct it even if it means considerable rewriting.

If there is a fact you cannot check but which a reader could know, leave it out and find another way of saying what it is you need. Don't ever guess if there's a chance you could be proved wrong.

Question everything. Authors often make mistakes because they think something is accurate, perhaps because they think they know it. Don't depend on your memory for facts, check them all.

Action point

Look through some past work and the notes which you made when doing it. See whether you have references to any facts, such as where you found them, or who said something on what date, or what reference books you consulted.

If anything puzzles you now, and you cannot verify a fact, make a resolution to be more precise in future and keep better records.

SPOTTING ERRORS

It is notoriously difficult to see your own mistakes. You are far too close to them and see what you expect to see, what you think you have written. This applies to simple spelling or typing errors and bigger faults, perhaps something that invalidates a whole argument.

Screen blocks

Many people find it more difficult to spot errors on a computer screen than on paper. This may change as we become more familiar with using screens, but if you do use a computer it often helps to print out your work and do revisions on paper. You can also do spell-checks on most word processing programs, which will stop silly mistakes reaching the publisher. But be wary: spell-checks will not pick up errors of meaning such as effect instead of affect, or practise instead of practice, since all are valid words.

Checklist: Correcting and changing

● Do you spot errors in your own work?

●   Are you reluctant to change what you have written?

Don't be in too big a hurry
One way to overcome this, once you have finished your first draft, is to put the work away for a while. If it is a topical article you have to supply for tomorrow's paper, then you obviously can't do this, but only experienced journalists are likely to be in this position.

   Most writing can be put aside for a short time. Make it as long as you can reasonably afford to wait, then reread it so that it is fresh to you. You could do something else in the meanwhile, and leapfrog the two projects.

Action point
Make a rough timetable for your next two projects, setting aside time for first drafts, revision and final polishing (see Figure 9).

TIMETABLE FOR WORKING AND REVISION

date	first draft	rewrite	polish
	project A		
	project B		
		project A	
		project B	
	project C		
			project A
		project C	
			project B
	project D		
			project C

Fig. 9. Outline timetable for working and revision.

TAKING ADVICE AND CRITICISM

The easiest way
A critique group is the commonest form of writers' group where work
can be read and opinions gathered. Some are very valuable, but they
have snags.

Be aware

● Unstinting praise can be very destructive. If it gives an author an
  inflated idea of his talent the inevitable rejection from a publisher
  can be a devastating blow.

● Attempts to mould writers into the image and style of literary lions
  are equally destructive. Writers need their own voices.

● Giving incorrect information is damaging.

● Telling a writer his work is rubbish is unkind as well as not usually
  true.

● Total rewriting demoralises the writer, teaches him nothing, and
  serves only to inflate the ego of the critic.

● Ignore anyone rewriting your work in his particular style, who adds
  to the wordage or changes the meaning.

Be constructive

● The most useful groups are those where the criticism is informed
  and constructive.

● The best criticism is the sort which makes suggestions on improving a piece without doing it for the writer.

● To say a section is boring may induce a writer to re-examine and cut
  it: to make the cuts for him doesn't help the writer learn to avoid
  being boring in future.

● To say more dialogue would be of help here is useful: to write the
  dialogue is not. For one thing a critic will not be able to keep to the

original writer's style accurately, for another he may be changing the meaning in a way the writer did not intend.

● Pay attention if several people make the same criticism and you think they may have a point.

Checklist: How do you take criticism?

1. Have you ever shown your work to anyone?

2. If so was it a fellow writer?

3. If not who was it?

4. If you have shown your work what response did you get?

5. If you have not shown your work, why not?

6. Can you judge others' work better than your own?

7. Do you think others can help improve your work?

8. To whose advice are you most likely to listen?

9. Does criticism of your work hurt?

Professional criticism

If you can pay for individual criticism of your work there are several agencies where it can be found. Since there are no recognised qualifications for this sort of work, try to go by personal recommendation.

Ask what you will get, whether there will be market advice, what experience your critic has in your particular type of writing.

It is your work

Remember it is **your** work, and can be damaged by unnecessary tinkering. Only you should make any necessary changes.

POLISHING

Revising and rewriting make the major changes which are needed.

Your last task before sending off a manuscript is to read it through one more time for a final polish. In your rearrangement of words, perhaps, you may have left in something no longer needed, or not changed the tense or case to match the new wording.

By now you may be so bored with the whole project all you want to do is pack it off and forget about it, but don't be too hasty. The final polish is worth while. It shows an editor you care about your work and are professional in your approach.

When you get to the end, stop

Polishing can go on endlessly and writers can be too perfectionist. This may sound odd, but it happens. It can stem from fear of rejection. Constant revision staves off the day when a publisher must be approached or the work shown to someone else.

Your writing must be done to the best of your ability but there comes a time when yet more changes and refinements can damage the freshness of the writing.

Your aims must be to:

● complete the work in a reasonable time
● revise it as much as you can
● believe in it.

CASE STUDIES

Yvonne tidies up

'You are improving a lot,' Yvonne's tutor tells her. 'If you cut this by half it stands a chance with a magazine for parents.'

Yvonne crosses out every superfluous word, spots several places where she's repeated information, and rephrases sentences to make them shorter and sharper. She checks that 'ise' endings are consistent, and confirms some facts by telephoning the education department and her local education authority.

To her delight it is accepted, but when it is published it has been shortened again.

'It was good as it was! Why have they cut it?' she asks.

'This feature is always in a single column.'

Yvonne has done well, but editors still have work to do.

Susan attends a writers' meeting

A writers' circle is formed in Susan's town and she decides to join. She takes a chapter of her new novel, a murder mystery, to the first meeting and reads it out.

'I prefer a murder in a locked room,' one member says.

'And having the detective telling the story,' another adds.

'I like the psychological approach,' a woman suggests.

'Have more detail about the victim before the body is found,' the first puts in.

'That wouldn't be my story, I'd have to change most of it.'

Susan resents these attempts to rewrite her story and change her style, so doesn't join the group. It wouldn't help her.

James steps back from his work

James remembers how he overcame a problem by taking a break. Until now he's done one thing at a time, polishing it until he is satisfied. It takes a lot of time, and often he finishes up back where he started.

'I can't judge it properly, I'm too close,' he says.

He plans his next three projects so that he can do the first draft of one, put it aside and start the next, and then revise the first, by which time he can see what needs changing. When he sends the first article off he begins the third, and continues leapfrogging so that he always has three projects in hand — rough outline, revising, and submitted.

He begins selling more work. Taking it slowly has paid off.

DISCUSSION POINTS

1. Most of us have some blind spots with spellings, and it may have been a long time since we had grammar lessons. Do you need to brush up your spelling and grammar, and how might you do it?

2. Find a piece of work to which you have made major changes, as in Figure 7. Can you identify why you made the particular changes, and whether you are still satisfied with them?

3. Do you need another opinion on your work? If so, do you know where best to find an objective critic?

10
Submitting Your Work

LAYOUT AND PRESENTATION

The traditional layout is typed, double spaced, on one side of good quality A4 white paper, with wide (at least 2-4cm) margins all round.

Paragraphs, apart from the first in a chapter or section, should be indented five spaces, with no lines left between paragraphs unless to indicate the end of a section (see Figure 10). This is so that the length can be estimated accurately for printing and costing purposes. In a book new chapters start on new pages, each page numbered consecutively through the entire script.

Cover sheet

It is wise to put your name and the title on each page but there should also be a covering sheet with your name, full address and telephone number, the title of the work, an estimate of the number of words, and an indication of which rights are being offered for sale. If there are any accompanying illustrations such as photographs these can be mentioned briefly (see Figure 11).

Make life easy for editors

The objective of a writer seeking publication is to give a favourable first impression. One way is to make life easy for the editor considering the script. Very faint lettering, a fancy typeface, or letters too small for easy reading will condemn your script, probably unread.

Editors read a lot and need to protect their eyes. Use ten letters to the inch of a clear type.

Don't stifle it

Put the script into a simple folder such as an envelope one, or hold the pages together with a rubber band and post in a strong, padded envelope. Short scripts or articles can be paperclipped and folded once only to fit into large envelopes.

CHAPTER THREE

'Don't worry, I'll go along an' see the poor lass this morning,' Phoebe said as she ladled out porridge.

'Will you bring her home?' Lizzie asked.

'No, she'll be better off at the hotel. Mrs Endersby wrote that we weren't to worry, she'd be well looked after.'

'I'll go to see her straight after work. It's on the Hagley Road, isn't it?' Josie offered.

'I'll come too. What about you, Freddy?'

'Poor Ann won't want too many visitors,' Freddy said hastily. 'Besides, I gotta see a man about a dog!'

'Oh no! I thought you'd given up that daft idea,' his mother said. 'You'll keep no pesky dog in my garden!'

Freddy grinned at her. 'I'll find somewhere, but one o' these days, Ma, you'll regret not takin' a share in me champion greyhound! When I'm drivin' me Rolls-Royce Phantom, smokin' cigars, expensive women by me side, you'll be kickin' yerself you don't share me good fortune!'

'Cheeky devil! You'd be better off lookin' for a job to do with motorbikes or cars, yer can manage them! Then yer might get ter drive a Rolls Royce.'

'I'm not slavin' over cars belongin' to other blokes.'

'At least you're not wearin' out shoe leather lookin' for a job,' she added sarcastically.

52

Fig. 10. Example typescript layout.

```
                         A. N. Author
                         Jasmine Cottage
                         Willow Lane
                         High Town
                         Midshire.
                         Tel: 012 345 6789




        MY LIFE WITH A FAMOUS DAUGHTER

                  BY

            ANNIE AUTHOR




Approx. 2,500 words
First British Serial Rights Offered
```

Fig. 11. Example cover sheet.

Never pin or staple sheets together or fix them into ring-binders or tie with convoluted nets of string and sailors' knots. Editors don't appreciate being stabbed or having to struggle to open or read a script.

Most magazines now accept computer disks with articles on them — but check first what format is acceptable and send a printed copy as well.

SUBMISSIONS, SUMMARIES AND PROPOSALS

Submissions

Submissions stand more chance of success if they are made professionally. Your work should conform to the standard layout but also to any special conditions an individual publisher expects.

Always send return postage on a self-addressed envelope or self-stick label. Publishers cannot afford to pay to return thousands of submissions.

Try to send work to an editor personally. Names can often be found in the yearbooks or you could ring the publisher to ask who deals with specific submissions.

How long to wait?

Unfortunately some busy publishers may take a long time to get round to unsolicited scripts. Occasionally a script is lost. A polite phone call six to eight weeks later can help.

Enquiry letters

Many publishers ask for an enquiry letter first. This information is in the yearbooks or you can telephone the publisher and ask what their policy is. If you send anything else it will probably come back unread and you'll simply have wasted the postage.

An enquiry letter should be one side of A4 paper, single spaced and businesslike. Say what you have written, with a brief three or four line summary, why you think it might be of interest to that publisher, whether you have had anything else published or have expertise in the subject. Specify the title and length (see Figure 12).

Try to make your letter stand out so that the publisher feels it would be worth while reading your script. You will be more successful by behaving professionally than by indulging in irritating gimmicks.

Partials

For novels publishers often prefer to see the first few chapters or 50 pages. If it is suitable they will ask to see the rest. An experienced reader can judge within a few pages whether the work is of the right quality and suitable for them. Sending a few chapters saves you postage. For non-fiction books it is more usual to send a proposal before starting the book seriously.

Multiple submissions
You can send copies to several magazines if you have a topical article, but tell them you have done so. Better still, ring round to ask who might be interested. Some book publishers also accept multiple submissions. Once an offer has been accepted you must tell the other publishers at once that the script is no longer on offer.

Summaries
This is the briefest possible description of your work, the bare essentials.

Examples
'This article is aimed at young mothers with toddlers and deals with the pros and cons of different types of childcare', or 'This is a novel about a marriage in France during World War Two, showing how it comes under attack during a time of exceptional strain and divided loyalties' will be enough to explain the background and the sort of article or novel it is likely to be. It tells an editor the crucial points and provides sales-men with a succinct description to give to potential buyers.

Writing a summary of other people's work is a useful exercise, making you select the most important features. Doing the same for your own work is equally instructive. If you hone and shorten the summary you will eventually condense it to what is the essence of the work.

Action point
Write summaries of the next ten books, short stories or articles you read.

Synopses
Be clear
A synopsis is longer. Many book publishers ask for them. About three pages, double-spaced, is a reasonable guide to length, but they can be shorter or much longer.

The synopsis should tell the story briefly, or with non-fiction detail the contents. They should include the important facts, in a novel introduce the main characters and their problems, and convey the style of your writing (see Figure 13). If they are interesting and exciting they may induce an editor to read the manuscript.

A N Author
Jasmine Cottage
Willow Lane
High Town
Midshire
Tel: 012 345 6789

1 January 199X

Janie Editor
Features Editor
My Own Magazine
The Twin Towers
London

Dear Janie Editor,

May I send for your consideration my article 'My Life with a Famous Daughter'?

It is 2,500 words, covering both the joys and difficulties of being the mother of a fifteen-year-old actress who is recognised everywhere. It includes hilarious incidents, heart-warming anecdotes, and tips on how to survive constant public attention.

The topic is dealt with seriously, covering real problems in a practical manner, and might fit into your 'Life With . . .' pages.

I have had published two non-fiction books on working abroad, several articles on that topic in both American and British magazines, and do a regular holiday and travel column for Midshire County Magazine.

Yours sincerely,

A N Author
sae enclosed

Fig 12. Sample enquiry letter.

Proposals

A proposal is more than a synopsis. It outlines the project. For a text-book this includes a list of contents, chapter headings, details about illustrations, what is needed and whether you can provide them, sample pages, and exercises where appropriate.

Suggest how it might fit into an existing slot in a magazine, or series of books or plays.

Say what the intended readership is, what has already been written about the subject, whether there are similar or rival books, or a gap your project can fill.

It may be suggested that an editor works with you from this stage on to give guidance.

Checklist: Planning and selling your work

● Do you plan to write non-fiction?

● Do you have ideas for books which could fit into an existing series, say picture books or stories for children?

● Can you plan a project in detail before writing it?

● Are you a competent salesman?

Action point

Look at a series of books you know or can find out about and see what gaps there are.

COPING WITH REJECTIONS

An incredibly small proportion of writers can boast they never had a rejection. They are fortunate ones who discovered what they wanted to write at once, were good at it, writing when it was in demand, sent it to the right editor at the right time and have maintained this success. In almost all cases they write long pieces, novels or textbooks, not short stories or articles.

Even established and successful writers receive rejections. Article writers reckon that selling half of their ideas is a good result. Once established, they write proposals and search for commissions, so the active writing is less than it might seem.

Synopsis of The Cobweb Cage by Marina Oliver

Marigold is caught in the web of her family, held by twin strands of love, and guilt which arises out of an accident to her youngest sister Ivy.

Life is hard in Hednesford, a Staffordshire mining village. Her father John is injured, her brother Johnny begins stealing from his employer, her sister Poppy is discontented, and Ivy clings, demanding attention.

Marigold escapes to a job in Oxford and meets Richard Endersby, son of a wealthy pottery manufacturer. Despite opposition and their vastly different social backgrounds they marry, but it is 1914 and Richard joins the Royal Flying Corps.

When Marigold's son is born Richard is missing in France. Calamity strikes when John is crippled. They face destitution until Marigold gives up her son in return for money to start a business, a hotel in Birmingham.

Richard, meanwhile, is in a German hospital until he escapes to Switzerland. Deceived into believing Marigold and his son are dead, he remains there.

The family gradually disintegrates until, during a fierce row, Ivy tells Marigold that Richard is alive. She finds him apparently happy and about to marry, and leaves without revealing her presence. Richard, on his way to America, looks for the graves of his wife and son. Instead he finds Marigold.

Fig. 13. A sample synopsis.

It doesn't mean your work is bad

A rejection is not a personal insult. It does not mean the work is bad or not worth publishing. There are many reasons an editor cannot use material. You may have sent it to the wrong publisher, or just after they have accepted something very similar, or have too much in hand to take anything else. Editors are human, have off days and personal preferences, so your work may simply land on their desk when they are not receptive, or it may not appeal to them.

Luck too

Much of this is luck. You can take precautions to make as certain as you can your work goes to the right editor, but at the start it is largely good fortune, given the ability to write well, if your work is accepted.

Once you have had an acceptance, though, take advantage of it. Cultivate that editor, send more work, write other material to suit, and build up a portfolio of successes you can quote in the future.

Persevere

Above all **don't give up**. If you don't learn and continue writing you will never succeed.

Checklist: Success and failure

● What is your response to failure — the impulse to give up or the determination to improve?

● What is your response to success — surprise, or a feeling of unshakeable confidence in the future?

Action points

1. Find out the names of the editors in your favourite magazines or book imprints.

2. Make a list of the names of editors you intend to approach with your work.

Famous last judgements
● 'Try the publisher down the road.' Frederick Forsythe, *The Day of the Jackal.*
● 'Animal stories don't sell.' George Orwell, *Animal Farm.*

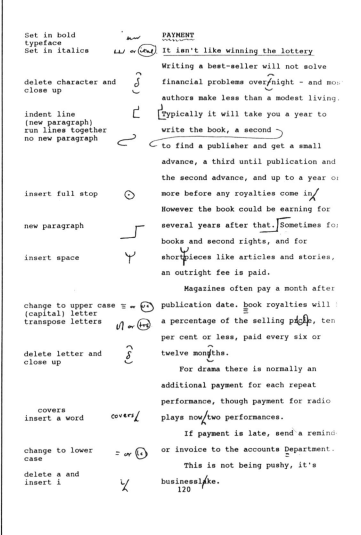

Set in bold typeface

Set in italics

delete character and close up

indent line (new paragraph)

run lines together no new paragraph

insert full stop

new paragraph

insert space

change to upper case (capital) letter

transpose letters

delete letter and close up

covers
insert a word

change to lower case

delete a and insert i

PAYMENT

It isn't like winning the lottery

Writing a best-seller will not solve financial problems overnight - and mos: authors make less than a modest living.

Typically it will take you a year to write the book, a second to find a publisher and get a small advance, a third until publication and the second advance, and up to a year o: more before any royalties come in

However the book could be earning for several years after that. Sometimes fo: books and second rights, and for short pieces like articles and stories, an outright fee is paid.

Magazines often pay a month after publication date. book royalties will a percentage of the selling price, ten per cent or less, paid every six or twelve months.

For drama there is normally an additional payment for each repeat performance, though payment for radio plays now two performances.

If payment is late, send a remind or invoice to the accounts Department. This is not being pushy, it's businesslike.
120

Fig. 14. Frequently-used proofreading marks.

96

AFTER ACCEPTANCE

Contracts
A contract can be a short letter or a multi-page document covering every conceivable possibility.

● *Read them*
Terms can often be negotiated, and this is where an agent is useful. The Society of Authors will give advice to members.

● *Ask for expert advice*
Longer contracts contain conditions such as who owns second rights, what proportions of future sales go to publisher and author, when the work will be published, what say the author may have over the jacket, how many free copies the author will get, disclaimers about unforeseen events which prevent publication, libel, copyright, and in what circumstances the book will be remaindered, that is when the copies left are sold off cheaply or pulped.

   If the contract is complicated get someone familiar with publishing to read it.

Proofreading
It is worth learning the most frequently used symbols used in proofreading, ready for when you are successful — as of course you are going to be (see Figure 14).

CASE STUDIES

Yvonne sends a query letter
'I'm tired of working so hard and having most of my articles come back,' Yvonne says despondently. 'I think the editors remember my first attempts and don't bother to read them.'

   'Magazine editors are far too busy for that. A rejection isn't a personal insult. Save time and send query letters.'

   Yvonne does this, and while there are still lots of rejections she hasn't wasted time on unwanted articles. She is asked to send a proposal and a sample article for a series.

   'They've commissioned me for six articles!' she reports to the next class. 'I'll have to work even harder now to prove I can do it, and perhaps they'll want more.'

   Yvonne is on her way to success.

Susan takes some good advice

To Susan's delight the publisher she sends her crime novel to is interested, if she agrees to make several biggish changes.

'I don't want to leave out that character, though,' she tells Mary, 'and they haven't offered much.'

'If you want to get published you'll do what they ask. But I think you ought to find an agent.'

'Why should I pay them?'

'They can argue terms for you, and advise on contracts. In the end you'll do better.'

Susan sees the sense of this, and while she is making the changes asked for she writes to several agents and one of them agrees to represent her. Susan has learned to take advice.

James becomes a columnist

'Look at this letter!' James exclaims. 'The editor of the county magazine wants me to submit ideas for a series of articles. They saw my piece on DIY disasters, and would like a humorous column each month. But I can't find enough to say about DIY mistakes!'

'They don't say it has to be DIY. Lots of funny things happen to gardeners too, and golfers and grandparents, all the things you know about. It sounds like a diary column.'

James heaves a sigh. 'Humour is hard work,' he says wryly, 'but it's a chance I can't miss. I don't think I'll play golf today, I'll go and work out some ideas as he asks.'

James is thrilled with his success, but knows he has to maintain his standards even more now.

DISCUSSION POINTS

1. Are you ready to submit some of your work, and do you know where? If not, why not?

2. How would you adapt the suggested enquiry letter in Figure 12 to make it a brief covering note for submissions?

3. When you write synopses and summaries of your work, what do you learn from the exercise?

Glossary

Acceptance. An offer to publish the manuscript.

Advance. Money given to an author by a publisher on signing a contract to write a book and/or on delivery of script and/or publication of that book.

Agent. A person or company that acts on an author's behalf, selling the author's work and negotiating fees. Agents take a percentage of authors' earnings.

Allowable expenses. Those expenses on machinery and equipment and essential requirements an author has in order to work, which can be offset against income before income tax is charged.

Angle. The way something is shown, which might be serious or funny, mysterious of straightforward, or the point of view it is written from.

Auctions. An agent will invite several publishers to bid for a script by a certain deadline. This happens with a few very important works.

Blockbuster. A large book of fiction, often aimed at the holiday market.

Blurb. A summary of the book which is printed on the cover or on the first page, and designed to attract readers.

Book jacket. The outer cover of the book, usually with an illustration.

Category fiction. Books/fiction of a particular type, *eg* romance or science fiction, which are published as a regular series and have similarities within the series such as length, style and conventions.

Contents. The list at the start of a book/magazine which shows the subjects covered and/or chapter headings and page numbers.

Contract. The terms agreed by author and publisher, covering such matter as payment, publication, ownership of second rights and proportions of earnings allocated under these.

Copy. A piece of writing sent to a magazine or newspaper.

Copy editing. Checking and altering a writer's work for the house style of the publisher.

Copyright. The legal rights an author/publisher has over their work, so that no one can copy all or part of the work without the author's or publisher's permission.

Cover sheet. The first page of a manuscript giving title, author, author's address and telephone number, and wordage.

Creative writing classes/courses. Often run by local authorities or educational institutions, they may be weekly sessions, day or weekend or longer.

Critique group. A group of writers who meet to criticise (hopefully constructively) others' work. Groups usually comprise amateur writers, but published writers do join.

Deadline. The date by which a writer aims to complete or submit a script.

Edition. A book may be published in different formats; each one is a separate edition.

Editor. The person who commissions writers for books/articles/plays and who sees the project through to the final printing and distribution.

Editing. Checking on accuracy, consistency, relevance, structure, and generally preparing a piece of writing for publication.

Enquiry letter. Letter to the editor outlining what an author has written, how long it is and why it might be of interest to the publisher.

Freelance. A writer who is self-employed and accepts assignments/projects from a variety of publishers and other sources.

Galleys. Typeset manuscripts in long columns, ready for proofreading.

Genre. A type of writing, *eg* crime, fantasy, historical, literary, romantic, saga, science fiction, western.

Hardback. Where the cover of the book is stiff.

Hook. The means by which a writer obtains the reader's attention and interest.

House style. Every publisher/magazine will have certain ways of writing things, for example standardising on spellings such as the use of 'ise' instead of 'ize' at the end of words like criticise.

Illustrations. Pictures, tables, graphs, diagrams, cartoons.

Large print. Editions of a book in a big typeface, intended to make reading easier for people with eyesight problems.

Layout. The way the writing is set out on the page, with margins, line spacing, headings.

Libel. A false, damaging statement published in permanent form.

Manuscript/script. An author's typed/word processed piece of work.

Market. Any place where a writer's work may be sold.

Moral rights. The rights of paternity, *ie* having one's authorship recognised, and of integrity, *ie* not having the work changed in a 'derogatory' manner. These rights have to be asserted in writing by the author.

Multiple submissions. Sending work to more than one publisher at a time.

Pace. The speed of progress, whether fast or slow, smooth or jerky, of a piece of writing.

Page proofs. Typeset manuscripts in page layout.

Paperback. A book the cover of which is flexible card or thick paper.

Partials. Part of a book which the publisher likes to see, in order to judge whether to read the rest with a view to publication.

Plagiarism. Deliberately to copy another writer's ideas such as plot and characters and use them as your own without acknowledgement.

Polishing. Checking a manuscript to make final changes and corrections.

Presentation. The way in which a manuscript is shown to an editor.

Printer. The machine which produces on paper documents stored in a computer. There are different types using different processes.

Program. The system by which a computer receives and deals with data.

Proofreading. Final check of galleys or page proofs for typos, spelling mistakes, missing text and so on.

Proofs. Typeset article/book which is corrected for printing.

Proof marks. The symbols used to indicate changes needed.

Proposal. Detailed outline of a project, together with a synopsis.

Public Lending Right. Money an author gets each time his book is borrowed from a library. The author must register for PLR at the time of publication.

Pulping. When books/magazines are sent back to the publisher/distributor because they are not bought, some are destroyed by reducing them to pulp which then goes to make paper.

Query letter. See enquiry letter.

Remainders. The books left after sales have fallen off are remaindered — offered to the author at a cheap rate and to cheap book shops.

Revising. Checking a piece of writing and making changes in it, including making sure the facts are accurate.

Rewriting. Changing a piece of writing, sometimes radically, sometimes with only minor alterations.

Rights. Legal rights of an author in terms of the sale of a piece of work.

Royalties. A percentage of the selling price of a book that goes to the author after publication, based on the numbers sold or the monies received.

Second rights. Editions of a book or article after the first publication, *eg* paperback, large print, translation, syndication, extracts, anthologies, adaptations for radio or TV or film.

Softback. See paperback.

Spread. Two pages facing one another in a book or magazine.

Sub-editor. The person who assists the editor in checking copy and getting it ready for publication.

Sub-editing. Checking copy for house style, accuracy, consistency, spelling, grammar and so on.

Sub-heading. An interim title used to break up a magazine article or non-fiction book, and separate and identify sections.

Submissions. The manuscripts sent to editors for consideration, in the hope of acceptance.

Summary. A three or four line outline of what a piece of writing is all about.

Syndication. When an article is published in several magazines or newspapers simultaneously.

Synonym. A word with the same or a similar meaning as another word.

Synopsis. A detailed description of a piece of writing.

Textbook. A book used for educational purposes.

Thesaurus. A book which gives alternative words of the same or similar meanings, and where concepts are often grouped.

Title page. Cover sheet of manuscript.

Trade paperback. A book with a flexible cover, but usually of a larger format and higher price than the conventional paperback.

Typeface. The style of the typed characters — there are many different typefaces and publishers will use different ones for different projects.

Typos. Typing errors on the manuscript or galleys.

Typesetting. Putting a piece of writing into the typeface, size and in the appropriate space (for example columns in a magazine) that the publisher uses.

VAT. Value Added Tax, imposed on almost all purchases, which can be reclaimed by persons registered under the scheme.

Voice. The particular individual style of a writer.

White space. The empty space at the ends of short lines and chapters.

Wordage. The approximate number of words in a manuscript, calculated by multiplying the average number per line by the lines in a page and the total pages.

Word processing. Using a computer in order to type work, and then being able to manipulate the information by inserting, deleting, moving text, changing the layout and many more processes.

Writer's block. When a writer cannot continue, through lack of ideas or motivation, exhaustion, or psychological difficulties.

Yearbook. A reference book published annually, such as *The Writers' and Artists' Yearbook* or *The Writer's Handbook*.

Useful Addresses

WRITING COURSES

Correspondence Colleges
These provide both general and specific courses:

The London School of Journalism, 22 Upbrook Mews, Bayswater, London W2 3HG. Tel: (0171) 706 3536. Fax: (0171) 706 3780.

The Writer's Bureau, Sevendale House, 7 Dale Street, Manchester M1 1JB. Tel: (0161) 228 2362.

Writers News Home Study Division, PO Box 4, Nairn IV12 4HU.

The Writing School, 29 Turnpike Lane, London N8 0EP. Tel: (0181) 342 8980.

Creative writing short courses
These are usually residential, are held in many places, including the following venues. As programmes change every year, contact the course organisers for details:

Alston Hall, Longridge, Preston PR3 3BP. Tel: (0177) 278 4661. Fax: (0177) 278 5835.

The Arvon Foundation, Lumb Bank, Heptonstall, Hebden Bridge, West Yorks HX7 6DF. Tel: (01422) 843714.

The Arvon Foundation, Moniack Mhor, Teavarran, Kiltarlity, Beauly, Inverness-shire IV4 7HT. Tel: (01463) 74675.

The Arvon Foundation, Totleigh Barton, Sheepwash, Beaworthy, Devon EX21 5NS. Tel: (01409) 23338.

University of Birmingham School of Continuing Studies, Edgbaston, Birmingham B15 2TT. Tel: (0121) 414 5615. Fax: (0121) 414 5619.

Burton Manor College, Burton, South Wirral, Cheshire L64 5SJ. Tel: (0151) 336 5172. Fax: (0151) 336 6586.

University of Cambridge Board of Continuing Education, Madingly Hall, Madingly, Cambridge CB3 8AQ. Tel: (01954) 210636. Fax: (01954) 210677.

The City Literary Institute, Room 24, Stukely Street, London WC2B 5LJ. Tel: (0171) 430 0542. Fax: (0171) 405 3347.

Creative Space, Lunga Mill, Ardfern, Argyle PA31 8QR. Tel: (01852) 5526.

Dillington House, Ilminster, Somerset TA19 9DT. Tel: (01460) 52427. Fax: (01460) 52433.

The Earnley Concourse, Earnley, Chichester PO20 7JL. Tel: (01243) 670392. Fax: (01243) 670832.

University of Edinburgh Centre for Continuing Education, 11 Buccleuch Place, Edinburgh EH8 9LW. Tel: (0131) 650 4400. Fax: (0131) 667 6097.

Fen Farm, Fen Road, Blo Norton, Near Diss, Norfolk IP22 2JH.

Knuston Hall Residential College, Irchester, Wellingborough, Northamptonshire NN9 7EU. Tel: (01933) 312104. Fax: (01933) 57596.

Lancaster University Summer Programme Office, The Storey Institute, Lancaster LA1 1TH. Tel: (01524) 382118. Fax: (01524) 849499.

Malham Tarn Field Centre, Settle, North Yorkshire BD24 9PU. Tel: (01279) 830331.

Maryland College, Woburn, Milton Keynes MK17 9JD. Tel: (01525) 290688.

Missenden Abbey, Great Missenden, Bucks HP16 0BD. Tel: (01494) 890295.

New Venture Holidays, 18 Old Chester Road, Bebington, Wirral, Merseyside L63 7LQ. Tel: (0151) 645 2532.

The Old Rectory, Fittleworth, Pulborough, West Sussex RH20 1HU. Tel: (01798) 82306.

The Poet's House, 80 Portmuck Road, Portmuck, Islandmagee, County Antrim BT40 3TP, Northern Ireland. Tel: (01960) 382646.

Rewley House, 1 Wellington Square, Oxford OX1 2JA. Tel: (01865) 270396. Fax: (01865) 270309.

St Andrews University Holidays, 66 North Street, St Andrews, Fife KY16 9AH. Tel: (01334) 62202.

University of Southampton Department of Adult Education, Highfield, Southampton SO9 5NH. Tel: (01703) 593469. Fax: (01703) 677642.

Suffolk College, Rope Walk, Ipswich IP4 1LT. Tel: (01473) 255885. Fax: (01473) 230054.

Summer Academy, University of Kent, Canterbury CT2 7NX. Tel: (01227) 470402. Fax: (01227) 784338.

Swanwick Writers' Summer School, The New Vicarage, Parsons Street, Woodford Halse, Daventry, Northants NN11 3RE. Tel: (01327) 61477.

The Talliesin Trust, Ty Newydd, Llanystumdwy, Cricieth LL52 0LW. Tel: (01766) 522811. Fax: (01766) 523095.

Trefechan Arts Centre, Pennant Melangell, Nr Llangynog, Powys SY10 0EU. Tel: (01691) 74346.

Urchfont Manor College, Urchfont, Nr Devizes, Wiltshire SN10 4RG. Tel: (01380) 840495. Fax: (01380) 840005.

West Dean College, West Dean, Chichester, West Sussex PO18 0QZ. Tel: (01243) 811301. Fax: (01243) 811343.

Westham House Adult Residential College, Barford, Warwick CV35 8DP. Tel: (01926) 624206. Fax: (01926) 624960.

Workshops and full-time training courses

These are offered in media jobs by the following:

London College of Printing and Distributive Trades, Elephant and Castle, London SE1 6SB. Tel: (0171) 514 6500. Fax: (0171) 514 6848. Training in journalism and printing.

London Screenwriters' Workshop, 1 Greek Street, London W1V 6NQ. Tel: (0171) 551 5570. Annual subscription £15. Offers workshop and criticism, plus newsletter.

National Council for the Training of Journalists, Latton Bush Centre, Southern Way, Harlow, Essex CM18 7BL. Tel: (01279) 430009. Fax: (01279) 438008. Runs training courses.

National Film and Television School, Station Road, Beaconsfield, Bucks HP9 1LG. Tel: (01494) 671234. Fax: (01494) 674042. Runs professional training courses.

Higher education and professional courses (BA, MA and Media Studies)

Lists of the courses run by universities and other specialist bodies can be found in *The Writers' and Artists' Yearbook*, and *The Media Guide*, a Guardian Book, published by Fourth Estate Ltd, 289 Westbourne Grove, London W11 2QA. Price £9.99.

PROFESSIONAL ASSOCIATIONS

Once you are published there are many specialist associations. Addresses or contacts can be found in writers' handbooks. Subscriptions sometimes vary for different categories of members, check before you send. There may also be separate charges for meetings.

*Associations that are open to unpublished writers.

Association of Little Presses*, 30 Greenhill, Hampstead High Street, London NW3 5UA. Tel: (0171) 435 1889. Membership fee £12.50. Publishers of a newsletter, poetry and little press information, catalogue of little press books in print, *Getting your Poetry Published, Publishing Yourself.*

The British Academy of Songwriters Composers and Authors (of lyrics)*, 34 Hanway Street, London W1P 9DE. Tel: (0171) 436 2261. Publishes a quarterly magazine *Buskers News.*

The British Amateur Press Association*, Michaelmas, Cimarron Close, South Woodham Ferrers, Essex CM3 5PB. Tel: (01245) 324059. For writers, editors, printers etc interested in writing/journalism as a hobby. Annual subscription £5.

The British Fantasy Society*, 2 Harwood Street, Heaton Norris, Stockport, Cheshire SK4 1JJ. Tel: (01614) 765368. For everyone interested in fantasy/horror. Publishes *British Fantasy Newsletter*, plus other annual booklets. Annual convention and awards. Annual subscription £15.

The British Science Fiction Association Ltd*, 52 Woodhill Drive, Grove, Oxon OX12 0DF. For anyone interested in science fiction. Publishes *Matrix, Focus* and *Vector* magazines. Annual subscription £12.

Comedy Writers' Association of Great Britain*, 61 Parry Road, Wolverhampton WV11 2PS. Tel & Fax: (01902) 722729. To assist and provide market information for comedy writers. Annual subscription £40.

Fellowship of Christian Writers*, Shee-Dy-Vea, 151A Bedford Road, Marston Moretaine, Bedford MK43 0LD. Tel: (01234) 767470. Manuscript criticism service and network of writers' groups available.

The Friends of the Arvon Foundation*, 6 Church Street, Darfield, Yorkshire S73 9LG. Publishes newsletter. Annual subscription £5.

Guild of International Songwriters and Composers, Sovereign House, 12 Trewartha Road, Praa Sands, Penzance, Cornwall TR20 9ST. Tel: (01736) 762826. Fax: (01736) 763328. Advice, guidance, assessment and collaboration offered. Publishes *Songwriting and Composing* magazine quarterly. Annual subscription £28.

London Writers' Circle*, Flat D, 49 Christchurch Street, London SW3 4AS. Meetings and workshops.

National Poetry Foundation*, 27 Mill Road, Fareham, Hants PO16 0TH. Tel: (01329) 822218. Advice, information, criticism and publishes a magazine. Annual subscription £16.

Networking*, c/o Vera Productions, 30 Dock Street, Leeds, West
    Yorkshire LS10 1JF. Tel: (01132) 428646. Fax: (01132) 451238. For
    women hoping to work in film, video or TV.
New Playwrights' Trust*, Interchange Studios, 15 Dalby Street, London
    NW5 3NQ. Tel: (0171) 284 2818. Fax: (0171) 482 5292. Offers
    scriptreading, workshops and information. Publishes newsletter.
    Annual subscription £15.
PEN International, for developing friendship and protecting freedom of
    speech. English PEN Centre, 7 Dilke Street, London SW3 4JE. Tel:
    (0171) 352 6303. Fax: (0171) 351 0220. Annual subscription
    (London) £30, (country and overseas) £25.
The Penman Club*, 185 Daws Heath Road, Benfleet, Essex SS7 2TF.
    Tel: (01702) 557431. Offers advice and criticism. Annual subscrip-
    tion £15 for first year, £8.25 for subsequent years.
Player-Playwrights*, St Augustine's Church Hall, Queensgate, London
    SW1; Secretary: 9 Hillfield Park, London N10 3QT. Tel: (0181) 883
    0371. Reads and performs members' plays. Annual subscription £5.
The Poetry Society*, 22 Betterton Street, London WC2H 9BU. Tel:
    (0171) 240 4810. Fax: (0171) 240 4818. Publishes *Poetry Review* and
    Poetry News. Offers information. Annual subscription £20 for
    London, £15 elsewhere.
The Romantic Novelists' Association*, 5 St Agnes Gate, Wendover,
    Bucks HP22 6DP. Tel: (01296) 623260. Offers criticism for unpub-
    lished members, plus meetings. Publishes newsletter. Annual
    subscription £20 plus £30 reading fee.
The Scottish Association of Writers*, 36 Cloan Crescent, Bishopbriggs,
    Glasgow G64 2HL. Tel: (0141) 772 5604. Organises conferences,
    competitions and workshops for member clubs.
Society of Authors, 84 Drayton Gardens, London SW10 9SB. Tel:
    (0171) 373 6642. Fax: (0171) 373 5768. For professional writers.
    Publishes quarterly journal *The Author*, plus guides on subjects like
    tax. Meetings and social events. Annual subscription £65.
Society of Women Writers and Journalists*, 110 Whitehall Road,
    Chingford, London E4 6DW. Tel: (0181) 529 0886. Meetings and
    advice services. Publishes quarterly newsletter. Annual subscription
    London £21, country £18.
Theatre Writers' Union*, c/o 1A Tower Street, London WC2H 9NP. Tel:
    (0171) 673 6636. Gives advice to playwrights, published or not,
    through regional groups. Publishes quarterly newsletter. Annual sub-
    scription variable.
Women Writers' Network*, c/o 23 Prospect Road, London NW2 2JU.

Tel: (0171) 794 5861. Monthly London meetings. Publishes newsletter and directory. Annual subscription £25.

Writers' Guild of Great Britain, 430 Edgeware Road, London W2 1EH. Tel: (0171) 723 8074. Fax: (0171) 706 2413. Trade union for writers.

OTHER USEFUL ADDRESSES

Arts Council of England, 14 Great Peter Street, London SW1P 3NQ. Tel: (0171) 333 0100. Fax: (0171) 973 6590.

Welsh Arts Council, 9 Museum Place, Cardiff CF1 3NX. Tel: (01222) 394711. Fax: (01222) 221447.

Scottish Arts Council, 12 Manor Place, Edinburgh EH3 7DD. Tel: (0131) 226 6051.

Northern Ireland Arts Council, 185 Stranmillis Road, Belfast BT9 5DU. Tel: (01232) 381591. Fax: (01232) 661715.

Regional Arts Councils: see lists in handbooks, or telephone directories.

The Association of Authors' Agents, 37 Goldhawk Road, London W12 8QQ. Tel: (0181) 749 0315. Fax: (0181) 749 0318. The professional body which has a code of practice.

Book Trust, Book House, 45 East Hill, London SW18 2QZ. Tel: (0181) 870 9055/8. Fax: (0181) 874 4790. Masses of information.

British Library Newspaper Library, Colindale Avenue, London NW9 5HE. Tel: (0171) 636 1544.

The Council for the Accreditation of Correspondence Colleges, 27 Marylebone Road, London NW1 5JS. Tel: (0171) 935 5391. Has lists of approved institutions.

Freelance Press Services, Cumberland House, Lissadel Street, Salford, Manchester M6 6GG. Tel: (0161) 745 8850. Fax: (0161) 745 8865. Agents for the US *Writer's Digest* books.

Public Lending Right, Baytree House, Prince Regent Street, Stockton-on-Tees, Cleveland TS18 1DF. Tel: (01642) 604 6099. Fax: (01642) 615641. All published books, all editions, should be registered and PLR money is distributed on the basis of library borrowings.

ADDRESSES OF DIRECTORIES

Check the prices before you send for them.

The Cottage Guide to Writers' Postal Workshops, Drake Myre Croft, Carin Orrie, Methlick, Ellon, Aberdeenshire AB41 0JN. Tel: (01651) 806252.

List of Literature Festivals, The British Council, 10 Spring Gardens, London SW1A 2BN. Tel: (0171) 930 8466. Fax: (0171) 839 6347.

List of Literature and Creative Writing, Short Courses and Summer Schools in Britain, The British Council, 10 Spring Gardens, London SW1A 2BN. Tel: (0171) 930 8466. Fax: (0171) 839 6347.

Residential Short Courses, booklet published annually, £4.25, by The National Institute of Adult Continuing Education, England and Wales, 19b De Montfort Street, Leicester LE1 7GE. Tel: (01162) 551451.

The Media Guide, a Guardian Book, published by Fourth Estate Ltd, 289 Westbourne Grove, London W11 2QA. Price £9.99. Has comprehensive lists of magazines, newspapers and broadcasting organisations plus telephone numbers for government offices, public organisations, pressure groups and business organisations.

Directory of Writers' Circles, Jill Dick, Oldacre, Horderns Park Road, Chapel en le Frith, Derbyshire SK12 6SY. Price £4 — make cheques payable to Laurence Pollinger Limited.

Further Reading

MAGAZINES FOR WRITERS

The Author, The Society of Authors, 84 Drayton Gardens, London SW10 9SB. Tel: (0171) 373 6642. £6 per copy or £15 per year.

The Bookseller, J Whitaker & Sons Ltd, 12 Dyott Street, London WC1A 1DF. Tel: (0171) 836 8911. Fax: (0171) 836 6381. £1.95 per copy or £108 a year. Main journal for the book trade.

Books for Keeps, The School Bookshop Association Ltd, Books for Keeps, 6 Brightfield Road, Lee, London SE12 8QF. Tel: (0181) 852 4953. £2.50 per copy or £15 per year. Review magazine for children's books.

Freelance News, (Journal of the Chartered Institute of Journalists' Freelance Division, SWC Media Services, 46 Ford End, Woodford Green, Essex IG8 0EG. Tel: (0181) 506 1011. Covers information of interest to freelancers.

Freelance Writing & Photography, 113 Abbotts Ann Down, Andover, Hampshire SP11 7BX. Tel & Fax: (0126) 471 0701. £17.70 per year. Information and hints.

Media Week, EMAP Media, 33-35 Bowling Green Lane, London EC1R 0DA. Tel: (0171) 837 1212. Fax: (0171) 837 3285.

Poetry Life, Poetry Life, 14 Pennington Oval, Lymington, Hampshire SO41 8BQ. Tel: (01590) 679269. Fax: (01590) 679269. £2 per copy. Helps new poets get recognition and publication. Has interviews with editors, publishers, festival organisers, poetry societies and famous poets for practical advice and tips.

The Woman Journalist, Barbara Haynes, 59 Grace Avenue, Maidstone, Kent ME16 0BS. Free to members of Society of Women Writers and Journalists. Articles of interest to professional writers.

Writers News, Writers News Ltd, PO Box 4, Nairn, Scotland IV12 4HU. Tel: (01667) 454441. Fax: (01667) 454401. Subscription £41.60 per year. Details of market opportunities, events, competitions, 'how to' articles, reviews and advice for writers. Also *Writing Magazine,* £1.80 per copy. 'How to' articles, competitions, market news, interviews and reviews.

Writers' Monthly, 29 Turnpike Lane, London N8 0EP. Tel: (0181) 342 8879. Fax: (0181) 347 8847. £33.50 per year. Information and advice for aspiring writers.

BOOKS ON WRITING

Some of the titles may be out of print, but should be available in libraries. New editions may be increased in price.

The main publishers of reference books for writers

Allison & Busby, 179 King's Cross Road, London WC1X 9BZ. Tel: (0171) 833 1042. Fax: (0171) 833 1044.

BBC Books, Woodlands, 80 Wood Lane, London W12 0TT. Tel: (0181) 576 2000. Fax: (0181) 576 2858.

A & C Black (Publishers) Ltd, 35 Bedford Row, London WC1R 4JH. Tel: (0171) 242 0946. Fax: (0171) 831 8478.

Blueprint, Chapman & Hall Ltd, 2-6 Boundary Row, London SE1 8HN. Tel: (0171) 865 0066. Fax: (0171) 522 9623.

Robert Hale Ltd, Clerkenwell House, 45-47 Clerkenwell Green, London EC1R 0HT. Tel: (0171) 251 2661. Fax: (0171) 490 4958.

How To Books Ltd, Plymbridge House, Estover Road, Plymouth PL6 7PZ. Tel: (01752) 735251. Fax: (01752) 695699.

Hodder & Stoughton Educational, Teach Yourself, Hodder Headline plc, 338 Euston Road, London NW1 3BH. Tel: (0171) 873 6000. Fax: (0171) 873 6024.

Elm Tree, Hamish Hamilton, Penguin Books Ltd, Bath Road, Hardmonsworth, Middlesex UB7 0DA. Tel: (0181) 899 4000. Fax: (0181) 899 4099.

Piatkus Books, 5 Windmill Street, London W1P 1HF. Tel: (0171) 631 01710. Fax: (0171) 436 7137.

William Heinemann, Reed Books, Michelin House, 81 Fulham Road, London SW3 6RB. Tel: (0171) 581 9393. Fax: (0171) 225 9424.

Routledge, 11 New Fetter Lane, London EC4P 4EE. Tel: (0171) 583 9855. Fax: (0171) 842 2298.

Reference books — general on writing and publishing

Writers' and Artists' Yearbook (A & C Black) £10.99. Lists publishers and magazines, plus gives advice on various aspects of writing and publishing.

The Writer's Handbook, Barry Turner (Macmillan Reference Books) £12.99. Another yearbook with lists and information.

The Author's Handbook, David Bolt (Piatkus Books).

Authors by Profession volume 2, Victor Bonham-Carter (Bodley Head). Volume 1 from the Society of Authors.

Inside Book Publishing: a career builder's guide, Giles N Clark (Blueprint).

An Author's Guide to Publishing, Michael Legat (Robert Hale). £6.95.

Publishing and Bookselling in the Twentieth Century, F A Mumby (Unwin Hayman).

Waterhouse on Newspaper Style, Keith Waterhouse (Penguin).

Willings Press Guide (Reed Information Services), Windsor Court, East Grinstead House, East Grinstead, West Sussex RH19 1XA. Tel: (01342) 326972. Fax: (01342) 327100. Information about publishers/magazines/books etc.

DICTIONARY AND THESAURUS PUBLISHERS

There are hundreds to choose from, you can select one to suit your pocket and need. Most publishers produce large, concise, compact, and pocket versions, hard and paperback. The major publishers are:

Cambridge University Press, The Edinburgh Building, Shaftesbury Road, Cambridge CB2 2RU. Tel: (01223) 312393. Fax: (01223) 315052.

Cassell plc, Wellington House, 125 Strand, London WC2R 0BB. Tel: (0171) 420 5555. Fax: (0171) 240 7261.

HarperCollins Publishers, 77-85 Fulham Palace Road, Hammersmith, London W6 8JB. Tel: (0181) 741 7070. Fax: (0181) 307 4440.

Helicon Publishing Ltd, 42 Hythe Bridge Street, Oxford OX1 2EP. Tel: (01865) 204204. Fax: (01865) 204205.

Larousse plc, Elsley House, 24-30 Great Titchfield Street, London W1P 7AD. Tel: (0171) 631 0878. Fax: (0171) 323 4694 and 43-45 Annandale Street, Edinburgh EH7 4AZ. Tel: (0131) 557 4571. Fax: (0131) 557 2936.

Longman Group Ltd, Longman House, Burnt Mill, Harlow, Essex CM20 2JE. Tel: (01279) 623623/426721. Fax: (01279) 431059/451946.

Oxford University Press, Walton Street, Oxford OX2 6DP. Tel: (01865) 56767. Fax: (01865) 56646.

ENCYCLOPAEDIAS

The publishers of encyclopaedias often publish concise or pocket editions as well as the larger versions.

The Cambridge Concise encyclopaedias, from Cambridge University Press, cost £7.95, £17.85.

The Guinness encyclopaedias, from Guinness Publishing Ltd, 33 London Road, Enfield, Middlesex EN2 6DJ. Tel: (0181) 367 4567. Fax: (0181) 367 5912. They cost from £9.99 to £35.

The Hutchinson encyclopaedias, published by Helicon Publishing Ltd, cost from £5.99 to £39.95.

The Macmillan encyclopaedias, from Macmillan Reference Books, 25 Eccleston Place, London SW1W 9NF. Tel: (0171) 881 8000 cost £9.99 and £24.99.

Pears Cylopaedia, from Pelham Books, Penguin, £14.99.

Wordsworth Encyclopaedia, Wordsworth Editions Ltd, Cumberland House, Crib Street, Ware, Hertfordshire SG12 9ET. £9.99.

OTHER REFERENCE BOOKS

This is just a selection, there are many more. Second hand copies of the annual publications can often be obtained at a fraction of the cost of new editions, and may serve your purposes quite adequately.

Brewer's Concise Dictionary of Phrase and Fable (Helicon) £8.99.

Brewer's Dictionary of Names, People, Places and Things (Helicon).

Cambridge Biographical Encyclopaedia (Cambridge University Press) £29.95.

Chambers Biographical Dictionary (Larousse) £17.99.

Chambers Dictionary of Spelling (Larousse) £5.99.

Chambers Dictionary of Synonyms and Antonyms (Larousse) £4.99.

Collins What Happened When (Helicon) £4.99.

Collins English Spelling Dictionary (Helicon) £5.99.

Concise Dictionary of English Idioms, B A Pythian (Hodder & Stoughton) £6.99.

Concise Dictionary of English Slang, B A Pythian (Hodder & Stoughton) £6.99.

Concise Dictionary of New Words, B A Pythian (Hodder & Stoughton) £6.99.

Concise Dictionary of Phrase and Fable B A Pythian (Hodder & Stoughton) £6.99.

Concise Oxford Dictionary of Proverbs (Oxford University Press) £5.99.

Egon Ronay's Cellnet Guide (Macmillan) £14.99.

Encyclopaedia of Dates and Events (Teach Yourself Books, Hodder & Stoughton).

Gascoigne Encyclopaedia of Britain (Macmillan) £29.95.

Good Hotel Guide Britain and Europe (Vermillion) £12.99.

Hutchinson Dictionary of Biography (Helicon) £12.99.

Hutchinson Pocket Fact Finder (Helicon) £7.99.

McNae's Essential Law for Journalists, Walter Greenwood (Butterworth & Co (Publishers) Ltd).

Oxford Dictionary of Modern Slang (Oxford University Press) £6.99.

Oxford Dictionary of Quotations (Oxford University Press).

Penguin Dictionary of Historical Slang, Eric Partridge (Penguin).

Penguin Dictionary for Writers and Editors (Penguin) £6.99.

Slang Down the Ages, Jonathan Green (Kyle Cathie) £16.99.

Whitacker's Almanack (J Whitaker & Sons Ltd).

Who Was Who, in 9 volumes plus index (A & C Black).

Who's Who (A & C Black) 1995, £90.

Wordsworth Dictionary of Foreign Words in English, John Ayto (Wordsworth Editions Ltd) £2.

ATLASES

Major publishers of atlases, often in conjunction with other publishing houses, are:

AA Publishing

RAC

Philips

Ordnance Survey

A to Z

REFERENCE BOOKS ON PARTICULAR FORMS OF WRITING

Children

How to Write for Children, Tessa Krailing (Allison & Busby) £6.99.

How to Write and Illustrate Children's Books, Felicity Trotman (Macdonald Orbis 1988) £12.95.

How to Write for Teenagers, David Silwyn Williams (Allison & Busby) £5.99.

The Way to Write for Children, Joan Aitken (Elm Tree, 1982) £6.95.

Writing for Children, Margaret Clark (A & C Black 1993) £7.99.

Writing for the Teenage Market, Ann de Gale (A & C Black) £8.99.
Writing for Young Children, Claudia Lewis (Poplar Press 1984) £4.95.

Creative Writing and General Books

Becoming a Writer, Dorothea Brand (Papermac) £3.95.
The Complete Guide to Writing Fiction, Barnaby Conrad *et al* (Writer's Digest Books (USA) 1990).
Conflict, Action and Suspense, William Noble.
Getting into Print, Jenny Vaughan (Bedford Square Press 1988) £4.95.
Get Writing, George Evans & Vince Powell (BBC Books 1990) £4.99.
The Book Writer's Handbook, Gordon Wells (Allison & Busby 1991) £6.99.
How to Get Published, Neil Wenborn (Hamlyn 1990) £2.50.
How to Publish a Book, Robert Spicer (How To Books) £9.99.
How to Publish a Newsletter, Graham Jones (How To Books) £9.99.
How to Write for Publication, Chriss McCallum (How To Books 1995) £8.99.
How to Write for the Religious Markets, Brenda Courtie (Allison & Busby) £6.99.
Is there a book inside you?, Dan Poynter & Mandy Bingham (Exley 1988) £6.95.
The 30 Minute Writer — How to Write and Sell Short Pieces, Connie Emerson (Writer's Digest) £11.95.
Research for Writers, Ann Hoffman (A & C Black) £10.99.
Revision, Kit Read (Robinson Writer's Workshop 1991) £5.99.
The Successful Author's Handbook, Gordon Wells (Papermac) £7.99.
Successful Writing, George Ryley Scott (Lloyd Cole 1993) £5.00.
Teach Yourself Creative Writing, Diane Doubtfire (Hodder & Stoughton 1993) £5.99.
The Way to Write, John Fairfax (Elm Tree) £8.99.
Ways with Words: BBC Guide to Creative Writing (BBC Books) £8.99.
Word Power — A Guide to Creative Writing, Julian Birkett (A & C Black) £9.99.
Writers' Questions Answered, Gordon Wells (Allison & Busby) £6.99.
The Writer's Rights, Michael Legat (A & C Black) £8.99.
The Writing Business, Liz Taylor (Severn House 1985) £3.95.
Writing for a Living, Ian Linton (Kogan Page 1988), £8.99.
Writing for Pleasure and Profit, Michael Legat (Robert Hale) £4.95.
Writing Popular Fiction, Rona Randall (A & C Black) £7.99.
Writing Proposals and Synopses that Sell, André Jute (Writers News).
Writing Step by Step, Jean Saunders (Allison & Busby) £5.99.

Journalism

The Craft of Writing Articles, Gordon Wells (Allison & Busby) £5.99.

The Craft of Food and Cookery Writing, Janet Laurence (Allison & Busby) £7.99.

Freelance Writing for Newspapers, Jill Dick (A & C Black 1991) £9.99.

How to be a Freelance Journalist, Christine Hall (How To Books) £8.99.

How to Sell Every Magazine Article You Write, Lisa Collier Cool (Writer's Digest Books (USA) 1986).

How to Write and Sell Interviews, Sally-Jayne Wright (Allison & Busby) £7.99.

How to Write and Sell Travel Articles, Cathy Smith (Allison & Busby) £6.99.

Interviewing Techniques for Writers and Researchers, Susan Dunne (A & C Black) £7.99.

Journalism for Beginners, Joan Clayton (Piatkus) £7.99.

Magazine Journalism Today, Anthony Davis (Heinemann Professional Publishing 1988) £12.95.

The Magazine Writer's Handbook, Gordon Wells (Allison & Busby 1993/4) £6.99.

1,000 Markets for Freelance Writers, Robert Palmer (Piatkus 1993) £9.99.

Successful Article Writing, Gillian Thornton (Writers News).

Teach Yourself Journalism, Michael Bromley (Hodder & Stoughton 1994) £6.99.

The Way to Write Magazine Articles, John Hines (Elm Tree) £8.99.

Writing Feature Articles, Brendan Hennessy (Heinemann Professional Publishing 1989) £12.95.

Writing for Magazines, Jill Dick (A & C Black 1994) £9.99.

Writing about Travel, Morag Campbell (A & C Black) £5.95.

Non-fiction

How to Write Non-Fiction Books, Gordon Wells (Allison & Busby 1996) £7.99.

Writing Your Life Story, Nancy Smith (Piatkus).

Novels

The Art and Craft of Novel Writing, Oakley Hall (Story Press (USA) 1994) £9.99.

The Art of Romance Writing, Valerie Parv (Allen & Unwin 1993) £7.99.

Bloody Murder Julian Symons (Penguin 1985) £3.95.

The Craft of Novel-Writing, Diane Doubtfire (Allison & Busby) £5.99.
The Craft of Writing Romance, Jean Saunders (Allison & Busby) £6.99.
Guide to Fiction Writing, Phyllis Whitney (Poplar Press 1984) £4.95.
How to Create Fictional Characters, Jean Saunders (Allison & Busby) £6.99.
How to Research Your Novel, Jean Saunders (Allison & Busby) £6.99.
How to Turn Your Holidays into Popular Fiction, Kate Nivison (Allison & Busby) £6.99.
How to Write a Blockbuster, Sarah Harrison (Allison & Busby 1995) £7.99.
How to Write Crime Novels, Isobel Lambot (Allison & Busby) £6.99.
How to Write a Damn Good Novel, James N Frey.
How to Write Historical Novels, Michael Legat (Allison & Busby) £5.99.
How to Write a Million, Dibell, Scott Card & Turco (Robinson Publishing Ltd 1995) £9.99.
How to Write Novels, Paddy Kitchen (Elm Tree Books 1981) £8.99.
How to Write Realistic Dialogue, Jean Saunders (Allison & Busby) £6.99.
How to Write Science Fiction, Bob Shaw (Allison & Busby) £6.99.
How to Write and Sell a Synopsis, Stella Whitelaw (Allison & Busby) £6.99.
How to Write and Sell Your First Novel, Oscar Collier with Frances Spatz Leighton (Writers' Digest Books 1995) £9.95.
Plotting and Writing Suspense Fiction, Patricia Highsmith (Poplar Press 1983) £4.95.
Writing Crime Fiction, H R F Keating (A & C Black 1987) £7.99.
Writing Erotic Fiction, Derek Parker (A & C Black) £8.99.
Writing Historical Fiction, Rhona Martin (A & C Black 1995) £8.99.
Writing the Novel from Plot to Print, Lionel Block (Writer's Digest Books 1979) £6.95.
Writing Science Fiction, Christopher Evans (A & C Black 1988) £4.95.
Writing and Selling a Novel, Marina Oliver (How To Books 1996) £8.99.
Writing a Thriller, André Jute (A & C Black) £9.99.
Write a Successful Novel, Frederick F & Moe Sherrard Smith (Escreet Publications 1991) £7.95.
To Writers with Love, Mary Wibberley (Buchan & Enright 1987) £4.95.

Poetry
The Craft of Lyric Writing, Sheila Davis (Writer's Digest Books (USA) 1986).

The Craft of Writing Poetry, Alison Chisolm (Allison & Busby) £6.99.
How Poetry Works, Philip Davies Roberts (Pelican 1986) £3.95.
How to Publish Your Poetry, Peter Finch (Allison & Busby) £6.99.
Songwriting, Stephen Citron (Hodder & Stoughton 1987) £14.95.
The Way to Write Poetry, Michael Baldwin (Elm Tree) £8.99.

Scriptwriting
The Craft of Writing TV Comedy, Lew Schwarz (Allison & Busby) £6.99.
How to Make Money Scriptwriting, Julian Friedman (Boxtree 1995) £11.99.
How to Write a Play, for the Amateur Stage, Dilys Gater (Allison & Busby) £6.99.
How to Write for Television, William Smethurst (How To Books) £8.99.
Screenwriting, Lew Hunter (Robert Hale) £12.99.
Screenwriting for Narrative Film and Television, William Miller (Harrap Columbus 1988) £7.95.
The Way to Write Radio Drama, William Ash (Elm Tree 1986) £8.99.
The Way to Write for the Stage, Tom Gallagher (Elm Tree 1988) £6.95.
The Way to Write for Television, Eric Paice (Elm Tree) £7.99.
Writing for the BBC, Norman Longmate (BBC Books) £3.99.
Writing for Film and Television, Stewart Bronfield (Simon & Schuster 1986) £5.95.
Writing a Play, Steve Gooch (A & C Black) £5.95.
Writing for Radio, Colin Haydn Evans (Allison & Busby) £6.99.
Writing for Radio, Rosemary Horstmann (A & C Black 1991) £6.99.
Writing Screenplays that Sell, Michael Hauge (Elm Tree) £9.99.
Writing for Television, Gerald Kelsey (A & C Black) £9.99.

Short Stories
How to Write Short Short Stories, Stella Whitelaw (Allison & Busby 1996) £7.99.
How to Write Stories for Magazines, Donna Baker (Allison & Busby 1995) £7.99.
Short Story Writing, Dilys Gater (Writers News).
The Way to Write Short Stories, Michael Baldwin (Elm Tree) £8.99.

Use of English
Creative Editing, Mary Mackie (Gollancz 1995) £8.99.
The Elements of Style, William Strunk Jr and E B White (Macmillan Publishing Co New York) £5.50.
Handbook for Written Language, Patricia Gordon (Hodder & Stoughton 1995) £3.99.

The Nuts and Bolts of Writing, Michael Legat (Robert Hale) £4.95.
Punctuation Made Easy in One Hour, Graham King (Mandarin) £2.99.
Teach Yourself Correct English, B A Pythian (Hodder & Stoughton) £5.99.
Teach Yourself English Grammar, B A Pythian (Hodder & Stoughton) £5.99.
Write Tight, William Brohaugh (Writer's Digest) £10.85.

Index

How to Get Into Films and TV
Robert Angell
Foreword by Sir David Puttnam

Would you like to make a career in films or television? Whether you want to direct feature films, photograph documentaries, edit commercials or pop videos, write current affairs programmes for television, do art work for animation or just know that you want to be involved in film or television in some capacity but are not quite sure how to set about getting started, this book will give you a wealth of information to guide you through the dense but exotic jungle of these exciting industries. Previous edition published as How to Make it in Films & TV. 'Readable and useful . . . At the back of the book is a useful section on writing letters/phoning/mailshots, and appendix and glossary.' *Amateur Film and Video Maker.* 'An indepth coverage of the subject. Offers a wealth of useful advice and addresses for more information . . . One of the essential references for careers libraries.' *The Careers Officer Journal.* 'A comprehensive guide in lay language . . . Each section includes suggested starting points for newcomers.' BAFTA *News.* 'Want to break into films and TV? Don't know how to go about it? Then look no further, for you'll find all the answers to your questions in Robert Angell's *How to Make It in Films & TV.* In it you'll find the various ways and means of getting into the industry, along with explanations of the various jobs available, and how they fit into the general pattern of film and programme-making.' *Film Review.* Robert Angell is a Council Member of the British Academy of Film & Television Arts (BAFTA) and Chairman of its Programme Committee and Short Film Award jury.

144pp illus. 1 85703 162 8. 3rd edition.

How to Be a Freelance Journalist
Christine Hall

Writing articles and features is a skill which can be learned by everyone with average ability and intelligence. Based on firsthand experience, this new book shows step-by step how you can break into print, how to develop your ideas into publishable articles, and how to sell them, and how to develop a profitable hobby into a fulltime freelance career. Written from the editor's viewpoint, this is an invaluable source of insider knowledge for writers at all levels. Christine Hall has wide experience as a subeditor, production editor, features editor, copy editor, deputy and acting editor for newspapers, consumer and trade magazines in the UK, Germany and China. A Member of the Society of Authors, and of the Society of Women Writers and Journalists, she has taught the craft of writing to beginners and advanced students alike.

160pp illus. 1 85703 147 4.

How to Write an Essay
Brendan Hennessy

This book will be an invaluable help to all students faced with writing essays, whether at school, college or university. Written by an experienced writing skills consultant and lecturer, the book explains the different approaches and techniques needed for essays in the humanities, social sciences and other disciplines. With the aid of examples, case studies and practical exercises, it discusses step-by-step how to choose the topic, how to research it, think about it, take notes, plan and compose the finished essay. The author also demonstrates how organising information, and using it to present coherent arguments and conclusions are skills which can be just as valuable in business, as in an educational setting. 'There is much good sense in this book.' *Times Educational Supplement.* 'If you're a student, buy it.' *Writers Monthly.*

176pp illus. 1 85703 159 8. 2nd edition.

How to Pass Exams Without Anxiety
David Acres

Now in its fourth and fully revised edition this is the best all-round exams handbook available for students on the market today. 'Must be high on the list of essential reading for all those involved in the matter of taking examinations . . . Written in crisp concise style with the text clearly laid out.' *Comlon* (LCCI). 'A specialist in study skills and techniques gives expert guidance.' *Teacher's Weekly.* 'Gives some very sensible advice.' *Focus on Business Education.* 'A thorough survey . . . easy to use, with checklists, summaries, reference headings and cartoons.' *Times Educational Supplement.* 'Good advice on revision and anxiety management.' *National Extension College.* 'Highly recommended.' *Open University.* David Acres is Learning Support Tutor at the College of Mark & John, Plymouth, and a specialist in study skills training and development.

168pp illus. 1 85703 174 1. 4th edition.

How to Write for Television
William Smethurst

Television is a huge and expanding market for the freelance writer. Particularly in the field of drama, producers are constantly looking for new writers for situation comedies, series drama, and soap operas and single plays. But what kind of scripts are required? How should a script be presented and laid out? What camera moves should you put in, and should you plan for commercial breaks? Which programmes and organisations should you contact, and which are the subjects to tackle or avoid? Packed with hard-hitting information and advice, and illustrated throughout with examples, this is a complete step-by-step manual for every writer wanting to break into this lucrative market. 'Packed with information which is well presented and easily accessible.' *National Association of Careers & Guidance Teachers Bulletin.* 'If would be TV scriptwriters are looking for a wide ranging and practical book to light the fuse which could lead to a successful career, they should certainly invest in a copy of William Smethurst's *How to Write for Television.*' BAFTA *News.* 'Your best starting point is probably William Smethurst's book.' *Writers News.* William Smethurst has written numerous scripts for both radio and television. He has been a television script editor at BBC Pebble Mill, and executive producer of drama serials for Central Television. He is now a director of the independent television company, Andromeda Television Ltd.

160pp illus. 1 85703 045 1.

How to Get Into Radio
Bernie Simmons

Between 1995 and 2005 we will see a huge expansion in radio stations, and digital audio broadcasting is set to revolutionise the industry. Radio broadcasting now offers an established career path, with industry-approved qualifications like NVQs and university degrees in radio broadcasting. There has never been a more exciting time to make a career in radio. But how do you get in? Where do you get started? What training is on offer? All this and more is revealed in this readable and up-to-the-minute new book. Bernie Simmons is a professional radio broadcaster with a wealth of varied experience. He himself started out in night club DJ-ing, hospital radio, and in-store radio. He has since worked on breakfast shows on independent local radio, news magazines and phone-in programmes on community radio, worldwide radio services such as BFBS Radio and The BBC World Service, Gold AM Radio and the pioneering Satellite Radio.

160pp illus. 1 85703 143 1.

How to Write Your Dissertation
Derek Swetnam

Almost all advanced educational courses now include a dissertation or research project of some type. For many students this can be a terrifying experience as the time for submission approaches and tutors are elusive. Although colleges and universities may have different systems, basic principles for planning research and making the inevitable compromise between what is desirable and what is feasible are the same. Some mature students may not have written extensively for years but it is assumed that they can cope with minimum help. This book offers a plain guide to ways of producing an excellent dissertation with minimum stress and frustration. It covers choosing a subject, planning the total work, selecting research methods and techniques, written style and presentation. The author is a former Course Leader of a large Master's level programme at the Manchester Metropolitan University with extensive experience of supervising students at all levels.

104pp illus. 1 85703 164 4.

How to Write an Assignment
Pauline Smith

Assignments play a large and increasingly valuable role in studying and learning in further and higher education. Written by an experienced tutor/lecturer, this book offers the student a clear framework for his or her own assignment-based work, and encouraging the development of such skills as information gathering, evidence evaluation, argument and presentation, which will prove valuable not only on educational courses, but in the wider workplace beyond. An experienced teacher, chief examiner and Open University tutor, Pauline Smith now lectures at Manchester Metropolitan University.

112pp illus. 1 85703 210 1. 2nd edition.